100 DELICIOUS DISHES
Rice & Pasta

New Orchard Editions
Poole Dorset

Edited by Isabel Moore

Published 1986 by
New Orchard Editions Limited
Robert Rogers House
New Orchard
Poole Dorset BH15 1LU

© Marshall Cavendish Limited 1986

ISBN 1 85079 065 5

Printed and bound in Italy by L.E.G.O.

Contents

DEPARTMENT OF CATERING
TELFORD COLLEGE OF F.E,
CREWE TOLL
EDINBURGH,

Key to symbols

⭐ This is a guide to each recipe's preparation and cooking

⭐ **Easy**

⭐ ⭐ **Requires special care**

⭐ ⭐ ⭐ **Complicated**

① This is a guide to the cost of each dish and will, of course, vary according to region and season.

① **Inexpensive**

① ① **Reasonable**

① ① ① **Expensive**

⧖ This is a guide to the preparation and cooking time required for each dish and will vary according to the skill of the individual cook.

⧖ **Less than 1 hour**

⧖ ⧖ **1 hour to 2½ hours**

⧖ ⧖ ⧖ **Over 2½ hours**

Basic metric conversions

Solid measures

15 grams	=	½ ounce
25 grams	=	1 ounce
50 grams	=	2 ounces
125 grams	=	4 ounces
225 grams	=	8 ounces
450 grams	=	1 pound
1 kilogram	=	2 pounds 2 ounces

Liquid measures

25 millilitres	=	1 fluid ounce
50 millilitres	=	2 fluid ounces
125 millilitres	=	4 fluid ounces
150 millilitres	=	5 fluid ounces
300 millilitres	=	10 fluid ounces
600 millilitres	=	1 pint
1 litre	=	1¾ pints

Linear measures

0·6 centimetre	=	¼ inch
1·3 centimetres	=	½ inch
2·5 centimetres	=	1 inch
10 centimetres	=	4 inches
15 centimetres	=	6 inches
23 centimetres	=	9 inches
30 centimetres	=	1 foot
1 metre	=	40 inches

American equivalents of food and measurements are shown in brackets.

Rice and pasta

Rice and pasta dishes were, not so long ago, firmly classed in the 'different therefore suspect' category by most of the English-speaking world. Occasionally, perhaps rice was used to make a warming pudding and pasta was legitimatized by the addition of a basic cheese sauce — but otherwise their potential was politely ignored and their popularity in other lands put down to foreign perversity.

Now, however, the word is out: the addition of staples such as rice and pasta to meat, fish and vegetables can eke out a meal, can make that end-of-the-week supper into an exotically acceptable dish, fit for any and all occasions. And economical needn't mean dull uninteresting cooking, as can be seen from a glance at the selection of recipes in this book — recipes such as hearty Russian Lamb Pilaff (pictured below, page 15), or Spaghetti alla Carbonara (page 46), a delicious mixture of pasta, bacon, eggs, cream and grated cheese.

And for those occasions when you've got people coming and don't mind spending a bit more time in the kitchen — well, rice and pasta can be festive too, as you can see from the colourful selection of recipes specially designed for worry-free entertaining — Lasagne (page 50), for instance, or Risotto alla Bolognese (page 28).

Any dishes that provide good eating at prices that won't empty your purse can only be welcome these days — and all of the recipes in this book are guaranteed to do just that.

Rice

Rice is one of the most important food grains in the world and is the staple food of millions of people. Cultivated rice, *oryza sativa*, has been known in India, where it is supposed to have originated, since about 3,000 B.C.

Rice is now produced in Asia, Africa, Latin America, parts of Europe, Australia and the United States. The latter is one of the world's largest exporters of rice; although the Asian countries grow a large amount, very little is exported as they require most of it for their own use. Most varieties grow on land submerged in water although there is a variety known as upland rice which grows well on dry land.

Because it keeps well, cooks more quickly and has a better appearance, most rice is milled before it is marketed. Milling removes the bran skin which lies under the husk, therefore some of the protein, minerals and vitamins are lost. Brown rice which has only the husk removed is more nutritious than other varieties and is often used in vegetarian dishes.

There are about 7,000 varieties of rice in almost as many colours — rice may be red, brown, blue, purple, black or ivory. Long, short and round-grain rice are the three most commonly used varieties in Western cooking.

Rice can be bought in several forms, among them are parboiled, pre-cooked (which only requires reconstituting in hot water) and boil-in-bag packs. Rice is also ground and used for puddings, or very finely ground to make rice flour for use in cakes and biscuits [cookies].

Wild rice, *zinzania aquatica*, is not a true rice, but a water grass which grows only in North America in swamps and shallow coastal waters.

Rice which is to be served as an accom-paniment for a curry or used to make a pilaff or biryani should be a long-grain variety such as Patna or basmati, the latter being the better. Risottos are best made with absorbent Italian rice such as avorio or crystalo. Round-grain rice is most suitable for rice puddings.

Rice absorbs liquids in varying amounts. Each variety, and sometimes different crops of the same variety, have unequal powers of absorption. The amount of liquid given in any recipe, therefore, can only be approximate. When cooking rice, check halfway through the cooking time and add more liquid if necessary.

Rice, when cooked, increases $2\frac{1}{2}$ to 3 times in bulk, so 1 cup of uncooked rice will yield between $2\frac{1}{2}$ and 3 cups of cooked rice.

Servings vary with appetite and custom but, on average, allow about $2\frac{1}{2}$ ounces [1 cup] of cooked rice per person.

BOILED RICE

To cook 10 ounces [1⅔ cups] of uncooked long-grain rice, wash thoroughly in cold running water. When the water runs clear, leave the rice to soak for 30 minutes, then drain.

Put the rice in a medium-sized saucepan. Pour over 1 pint [2½ cups] of water and add 1 teaspoon of salt. Place the pan over high heat and bring the water to the boil. Cover the pan, reduce the heat to low and simmer for 15 to 20 minutes or until the rice is tender and all the liquid has been absorbed.

FRIED RICE

In a large frying-pan, heat 3 tablespoons of vegetable oil over moderately high heat. When the oil is very hot, add 3 lightly beaten eggs. Before the eggs set too firmly, add 1¼ pounds [8 cups] cold, cooked long-grain rice and ½ teaspoon of salt. Fry, stirring constantly, for 3 to 4 minutes or until all the grains of rice are coated with the oil. (Other ingredients such as diced cooked ham and spring onions [scallions] may be added at this point to make a more substantial dish.)

Italian rice is cooked in a completely different way. It is a thick, short-grain, highly absorbent rice and requires slow cooking. The liquid is added a little at a time, the first amount being absorbed before more is added. (See recipe for Green Rice on page 8.)

BASIC RICE PUDDING

Preheat the oven to cool 300°F (Gas Mark 2, 150°C). Grease a 2-pint [1½-quart] baking dish with 2 teaspoons of butter. Place 1½ ounces [¼ cup] of round-grain rice, 2 tablespoons sugar, 1½ pints [3¾ cups] milk and 1 teaspoon vanilla essence or ⅛ teaspoon grated nutmeg in the dish. Place the dish in the oven and bake the pudding for 3 hours. If a richer pudding is required, beat in 2 egg yolks 30 minutes before the end of the cooking

1 Brown rice 2 Avorio rice 3 Basmati rice 4 Wild rice 5 Round-grain rice 6 Ground rice 7 Rice flour 8 Natural rice 9 Rice paper, similar in name only, comes from an Asiatic tree.

time. For a more attractive appearance remove the dish from the oven, sprinkle the top of the pudding with 1 tablespoon of sugar and place the dish under a hot grill [broiler] for 1 minute to glaze.

Rice with Aubergine [Eggplant] and Potatoes

An adaptation of a recipe from the west coast of India, Rice with Aubergine [Eggplant] and Potatoes may be served as a filling accompaniment to curries or roast pork.

6 SERVINGS

10 oz. [1⅔ cups] long-grain rice, washed, soaked in cold water for 30 minutes and drained
1 pint [2½ cups] water
1½ teaspoons salt
1 teaspoon turmeric
1 teaspoon ground cumin
1 tablespoon ground coriander
½ teaspoon cayenne pepper
½ teaspoon sugar
1 tablespoon lemon juice
2 teaspoons chick-pea flour
2 oz. [¼ cup] butter
12 oz. potatoes, peeled and cut into ½-inch cubes
1 large aubergine [eggplant], cubed and dégorged
2 oz. [¼ cup] butter, melted

Put the rice in a large saucepan. Pour over the water and add 1 teaspoon of the salt. Bring to the boil over high heat. Cover the pan, reduce the heat to low and simmer for 15 to 20 minutes or until the rice is tender and all the water has been absorbed. Remove the pan from the heat. Set aside and keep warm.

Meanwhile, in a small mixing bowl, mix the turmeric, cumin, coriander, cayenne, sugar, lemon juice, chick-pea flour and the remaining salt to a paste, adding more lemon juice if necessary. Set aside.

Preheat the oven to moderate 350°F (Gas Mark 4, 180°C).

In a large frying-pan, melt the butter over moderate heat. When the foam subsides, add the potato and aubergine [eggplant] cubes and fry, stirring frequently, for 5 minutes. Add the spice paste and fry, stirring constantly, for 10 minutes, adding a spoonful or two of water if the mixture becomes too dry. Cover the pan, reduce the heat to low and cook the vegetables for 15 to 20 minutes or until they are tender when pierced with the point of a sharp knife. Remove the pan from the heat and set aside.

Spread half the rice over the bottom of an ovenproof dish. Sprinkle 1 ounce [2 tablespoons] of the melted butter over the rice. Spread the vegetable mixture over the rice and cover with the remaining rice. Sprinkle the remaining melted butter over the top.

Cover the dish and place it in the centre of the oven. Cook for 20 to 25 minutes or until all of the ingredients are very hot.

Remove the dish from the oven and serve the mixture immediately, straight from the dish.

Brazilian Rice

This is a tasty and simple Brazilian way of cooking rice. It may be served instead of plain boiled rice with roast chicken or grilled [broiled] steaks.

4-6 SERVINGS

  4 tablespoons olive oil
  1 medium-sized onion, thinly sliced
12 oz. [2 cups] long-grain rice, washed, soaked in cold water for 30 minutes and drained
  2 tomatoes, blanched, peeled and chopped
  1 teaspoon salt
1¼ pints [3⅛ cups] boiling water

In a large saucepan, heat the oil over moderate heat. Add the onion and fry, stirring constantly, for 5 to 7 minutes or until the onion is soft and translucent but not brown. Add the rice and fry for 5 minutes, stirring constantly.

Add the tomatoes and salt. Cook for 2 minutes and then pour in the boiling water.

Reduce the heat to low, cover the pan and simmer for 15 to 20 minutes, or until the rice is cooked and all the liquid has

Rice with Aubergine [Eggplant] and Potatoes is an exotic accompaniment to meat curries.

been absorbed.

Turn the rice into a warmed serving dish and serve immediately.

Russian Rice

This dish from the USSR is delicately flavoured with sesame seeds and a little ginger. It makes an excellent accompaniment to roast chicken, roast lamb or a hot curry.

4 SERVINGS

  2 oz. [¼ cup] butter
10 oz. [1⅔ cups] long-grain rice, washed, soaked in cold water for 30 minutes and drained
  ½ teaspoon ground ginger
1½ teaspoons sesame seeds
  1 pint [2½ cups] chicken stock
  ½ teaspoon salt
  ½ teaspoon freshly ground black pepper
  2 oz. [½ cup] slivered, toasted almonds

Preheat the oven to moderate 350°F (Gas Mark 4, 180°C).

In a flameproof casserole, melt the butter over moderate heat. Add the rice and cook for 10 minutes, stirring constantly. Add the ginger and sesame seeds and cook for 3 minutes. Pour in the stock, salt and pepper and bring to the boil, stirring constantly.

Put the casserole in the oven, uncovered, for 35 minutes or until all the liquid is absorbed and the rice is cooked. Toss the rice with a fork after 10 minutes and again after 20 minutes. Taste and add more salt if necessary. Sprinkle with the almonds and serve immediately.

Saffron Rice

Aromatic Saffron Rice is an Indian dish which may be served as part of an Indian meal, or with kebabs and yogurt.

4-6 SERVINGS

  2 oz. [¼ cup] butter
    seeds of 4 whole cardamom pods
  4 cloves
  3 x 1-inch pieces cinnamon stick
  1 medium-sized onion, finely chopped
12 oz. [2 cups] long-grain rice, washed, soaked in cold water for 30 minutes and drained
1¼ pints [3⅛ cups] home-made boiling chicken stock
  1 teaspoon salt
  ¾ teaspoon crushed saffron threads, soaked in 2 tablespoons boiling

water for 20 minutes

In a medium-sized saucepan, melt the butter over moderate heat. When the foam subsides, add the cardamom seeds, cloves and cinnamon sticks to the pan and fry, stirring constantly, for 2 minutes.

Add the onion and fry, stirring occasionally, for 8 to 10 minutes or until it is golden brown. Add the rice, reduce the heat to moderately low and fry gently, stirring constantly, for 5 minutes.

Pour the boiling stock over the rice, add the salt and stir in the saffron mixture.

Cover the pan, reduce the heat to low and cook for 15 to 20 minutes or until the rice is tender and all the liquid has been absorbed. Remove and discard the cinnamon sticks.

Remove the pan from the heat. Spoon the rice on to a warmed serving platter and serve immediately.

Yellow Rice

This simple dish of rice flavoured and coloured with turmeric is a good accompaniment for roast chicken or lamb, or any strongly flavoured beef dish. Use a good quality long-grain rice such as basmati. If basmati is not available use any rice you are familiar with and alter the amount of water used accordingly.

4-6 SERVINGS

  2 oz. [¼ cup] butter
12 oz. [2 cups] long-grain rice, washed, soaked in cold water for 30 minutes and drained
  1 teaspoon turmeric
  1 teaspoon salt
  3 oz. [½ cup] sultanas or seedless raisins
  1 cinnamon stick
  1 bay leaf
1¼ pints [3⅛ cups] boiling water

In a medium-sized saucepan, melt the butter over moderate heat. When the foam subsides, add the rice. Reduce the heat to moderately low and, stirring constantly, fry the rice gently for 5 minutes. Add the turmeric, salt, sultanas or seedless raisins, cinnamon stick and bay leaf and stir well to mix.

Pour in the boiling water and increase the heat to moderately high. When the rice is bubbling, cover the pan, reduce the heat to low and cook the rice for 15 to 20 minutes or until it is tender and all the water has been absorbed. Remove and discard both the bay leaf and cinnamon stick.

Turn the rice into a warmed serving dish and serve.

African Vegetable Rice

This appetizing vegetable rice dish from West Africa makes an ideal light supper or lunch dish. It also makes an excellent stuffing for joints of meat or poultry.

2-3 SERVINGS

12 oz. [2 cups] long-grain rice, washed, soaked in cold water for 30 minutes and drained
1¼ pints [3⅛ cups] water
2 teaspoons salt
2 oz. [¼ cup] butter
1 medium-sized onion, finely chopped
2 large tomatoes, blanched, peeled and chopped
1 large red pepper, white pith removed, seeded and finely chopped
2 celery stalks, trimmed and finely chopped
4 oz. broccoli, trimmed and chopped
4 oz. mushrooms, wiped clean and finely chopped
¼ teaspoon cayenne pepper

Put the rice in a large saucepan. Pour over the water and add 1½ teaspoons of the salt.

Place the pan over moderately high heat and bring the water to the boil. Cover the pan, reduce the heat to low and simmer the rice for 15 to 20 minutes or until all the liquid has been absorbed and the rice is tender. Remove the pan from the heat and set aside.

In a large frying-pan, melt the butter over moderate heat. When the foam subsides, add the onion and fry, stirring occasionally, for 5 to 7 minutes or until it is soft and translucent but not brown. Add the tomatoes, red pepper, celery and broccoli. Fry, stirring frequently, for 10 minutes or until the vegetables begin to soften. Add the mushrooms to the pan and fry, stirring frequently, for a further 3 minutes. Season with the remaining salt and the cayenne.

Add the rice to the pan and stir the mixture until it is combined. Cook, stirring frequently, for a further 10 minutes or until the mixture is thoroughly heated through.

Remove the pan from the heat and serve at once.

African Vegetable Rice makes an appetizing light supper, or an unusual stuffing for poultry.

Balkan Chicken Pilaff

This pilaff depends on a strong chicken stock for its flavour. For convenience, cook the chicken and make the stock the day before. Serve the pilaff for a delicious family supper with ratatouille and a salad of yogurt with chopped cucumber and mint leaves.

6-8 SERVINGS

STOCK
1 x 3 lb. chicken
1 teaspoon salt
1 medium-sized onion, halved
2 carrots, scraped
4 peppercorns
PILAFF
3 oz. [⅜ cup] butter
1 medium-sized onion, finely chopped
3 tomatoes, blanched, peeled and chopped
1 teaspoon salt
½ teaspoon freshly ground black pepper
2 teaspoons chopped fresh basil or 1 teaspoon dried basil
2 oz. [⅓ cup] walnuts, chopped
1 lb. [2⅔ cups] long-grain rice, washed, soaked in cold water for

30 minutes and drained

First make the stock. Put the chicken in a pot large enough to hold it comfortably. Pour in enough water to come halfway up the sides. Add the salt, onion, carrots and peppercorns and bring to the boil. Reduce the heat to low and simmer the chicken for 1¼ hours or until it is tender and cooked. Remove the saucepan from the heat and let the chicken cool.

When the chicken is cool enough to handle, remove it from the stock. Put it on a board and cut off all the meat. Put the meat in a bowl, cover and place in the refrigerator.

Return the chicken bones to the pan, adding more water if necessary to cover, and simmer for 1½ hours. Strain the stock into a bowl, cool, cover and refrigerate. When the fat hardens on the top of the stock, skim it off with a spoon.

To make the pilaff, heat 1½ pints [3¾ cups] of the stock until it boils. Cut the chicken meat into bite-sized pieces.

In a large flameproof casserole, melt the butter over moderate heat. Add the chopped onion and fry for 8 minutes. Add the chicken pieces, stir and cook for 2 minutes. Add the tomatoes, salt, pepper, basil and walnuts and cook for 1 minute. Add the rice and cook for 2 minutes, stirring constantly. Pour in the hot stock, raise the heat to high and bring the rice to the boil. When it is bubbling briskly,

cover, reduce the heat to low and simmer for 15 to 20 minutes, or until all the liquid is absorbed and the rice is tender. Serve at once, straight from the casserole.

Chicken Pilaff

☆   ①

The tastiest way to make this dish is to use a whole chicken so that you can make the stock from the carcass and giblets. If you do not have the time to do this, chicken pieces and a stock cube will do, though the flavour of the pilaff will not be as good.

4 SERVINGS

2 oz. [¼ cup] butter
1 x 4 lb. chicken, cut into serving pieces, or 8 chicken pieces
1 teaspoon salt
½ teaspoon freshly ground black pepper
1 teaspoon chopped fresh tarragon or ½ teaspoon dried tarragon
8 oz. button mushrooms, wiped clean
12 oz. [2 cups] long-grain rice, washed, soaked in cold water for 30 minutes and drained
1 pint [2½ cups] home-made chicken stock
5 fl. oz. single cream [⅝ cup light cream]

In a large saucepan, melt the butter over

This delicately creamy Chicken Pilaff is best made with home-made stock, but you can save time and use a stock cube and water. Serve with a tossed mixed salad, crusty bread and lots of ice-cold lager.

moderate heat. When the foam subsides, add the chicken pieces and cook them, turning them frequently, for 6 to 8 minutes or until they are lightly browned. Sprinkle the chicken pieces with half of the salt, the pepper and tarragon. Reduce the heat to low, cover the pan and cook the chicken pieces, turning occasionally, for 35 minutes.

Uncover the pan, increase the heat to moderate and add the mushrooms. Continue cooking for 10 minutes, stirring occasionally.

Add the drained rice and the remaining salt and cook, stirring constantly, for 5 minutes.

Pour in the chicken stock and bring the mixture to the boil. Cover the pan, reduce the heat to low and cook the pilaff for 15 to 20 minutes or until the rice is tender and all the liquid has been absorbed, and the chicken pieces are tender when pierced with the point of a sharp knife. Remove the pan from the heat and stir in the cream.

Spoon the pilaff on to a warmed serving platter, and serve immediately.

Chicken Liver Risotto

Tasty and inexpensive, Chicken Liver Risotto is very simple to prepare and ideal to serve as a main dish for lunch or supper accompanied by a green salad.

4 SERVINGS

2 oz. [¼ cup] butter
1 onion, finely chopped
4 oz. mushrooms, wiped clean and sliced
10 oz. [1⅔ cups] long-grain rice, washed, soaked in cold water for 30 minutes and drained
1 pint [2½ cups] boiling chicken stock
8 chicken livers, cut into small pieces
2 tablespoons chopped fresh parsley
2 oz. [½ cup] Parmesan cheese, grated

In a large, heavy saucepan, melt three-quarters of the butter over moderate heat. Add the onion and cook, stirring occasionally, for 5 to 7 minutes or until the onion is soft and translucent but not brown. Add the mushrooms and cook for a further 3 minutes.

Add the rice to the saucepan and cook, stirring constantly, for 2 minutes. Pour on the stock and let the rice cook over high heat for 15 seconds. Cover the saucepan, reduce the heat to low and simmer gently for 15 to 20 minutes, or until the liquid is absorbed and the rice is tender.

While the rice is cooking, prepare the chicken livers. In a medium-sized frying-pan, melt the remaining butter over moderate heat. Add the chicken livers and cook them for 10 minutes, stirring

occasionally.

When the rice is cooked, stir in the chicken livers and parsley. Put the mixture into a warmed serving dish and sprinkle on the Parmesan cheese. Serve immediately.

Rice Croquettes

These tasty rice and shrimp croquettes may be served with a hot tomato sauce for a superb dinner.

4 SERVINGS

1 oz. [2 tablespoons] butter
1 oz. [¼ cup] flour
4 fl. oz. double cream [½ cup heavy cream]
1 teaspoon salt
1 teaspoon black pepper
¼ teaspoon hot chilli powder
1 tablespoon ground coriander
1 teaspoon garam masala
1 tablespoon tomato purée
8 oz. [3 cups] cooked long-grain rice
4 tablespoons canned sweetcorn
8 oz. peeled frozen shrimps, thawed and drained
1 egg, lightly beaten
4 oz. [1⅓ cups] dry white breadcrumbs
4 fl. oz. [½ cup] vegetable oil

In a large saucepan, melt the butter over moderate heat. Remove the pan from the heat and, using a wooden spoon, stir in the flour to make a smooth paste. Gradually add the cream, stirring constantly and being careful to avoid lumps.

Chicken Liver Risotto is super to eat, easy to prepare and it makes an inexpensive family supper dish.

Return the pan to the heat and cook the sauce, stirring constantly, for 2 to 3 minutes or until it is very thick. Stir in the salt, pepper, chilli powder, coriander, garam masala and tomato purée. Cook the sauce, stirring constantly, for a further 2 minutes.

Remove the pan from the heat and stir in the rice, sweetcorn and shrimps. Combine the mixture thoroughly and then chill it in the refrigerator for 1 hour.

Remove the pan from the refrigerator. Place the egg on one plate and the bread-crumbs on another. Break off pieces of the mixture and shape them into balls. Slightly flatten the balls between the palms of your hands and roll them, first in the egg and then in the breadcrumbs, coating them thoroughly and shaking off any excess crumbs.

In a large, heavy-based frying-pan, heat the oil over moderate heat. When the oil is hot, add half the croquettes and fry them for 3 to 4 minutes on each side or until they are heated through and crisp and golden on the outside.

Using a fish slice or spatula, transfer the croquettes from the pan to kitchen paper towels to drain. Arrange the croquettes on a warmed serving dish and keep them hot while you fry and drain the remaining croquettes in the same way.

When all the croquettes have been fried, serve immediately.

Green Rice

This delicious and very attractive Italian dish may be served for supper with a tomato salad.

4 SERVINGS

2½ oz. [5 tablespoons] butter
6 oz. [1 cup] Italian rice, such as avorio
15 fl. oz. [1⅞ cups] chicken stock
3 teaspoons salt
1 lb. fresh green peas, shelled
7 fl. oz. [⅞ cup] water
2 lb. spinach, thoroughly washed
1 teaspoon black pepper
1 teaspoon chopped fresh basil
1 teaspoon chopped fresh marjoram
2 oz. [½ cup] Parmesan cheese, grated

In a large saucepan, melt 1 ounce [2 tablespoons] of butter over moderate heat. When the foam subsides, add the rice and fry, stirring constantly, for 1 minute. Pour over about one-third of the stock and 1 teaspoon of salt. Regulate the heat so that the rice is bubbling all the time. Stir the rice occasionally with a fork. When the rice swells and the liquid is absorbed, add another one-third of the stock. Continue cooking the rice in this way until it is tender and moist but still firm.

Meanwhile, in a medium-sized saucepan, cook the peas with the water and 1 teaspoon of salt over moderate heat for 8 minutes, or until they are tender. Drain the peas and set them aside.

In another medium-sized saucepan, cook the spinach with the remaining salt over moderate heat for 7 to 12 minutes, or until it is just tender. Do not add any water because there should be enough left on the spinach leaves after they are washed.

Drain the spinach, pressing down with a wooden spoon to extract any excess liquid. Chop the spinach and sprinkle with the pepper. Arrange one-third on the bottom of a shallow heatproof dish.

When the rice is cooked add 1 ounce [2 tablespoons] of the butter, the basil and marjoram and toss until the rice is well coated. Spoon one-third over the spinach.

Purée the peas in a blender or mash them through a strainer. Spread one-third of the pea purée over the rice. Continue making layers of spinach, rice and peas, until all the ingredients have been used up.

Preheat the grill [broiler] to high.

Sprinkle the cheese over the top and dot with the remaining butter, cut into small pieces. Place the dish under the grill [broiler]. Grill [broil] for 3 to 4 minutes, or until the cheese is bubbling and beginning to brown. Serve at once.

Ham and Fried Rice

A delicious dish, cooked quickly in the Chinese way, Ham and Fried Rice may be served for supper or as part of a Chinese meal. Serve with a cucumber and tomato salad.

3-4 SERVINGS

8 oz. [1⅓ cups] long-grain rice, washed, soaked in cold water for 30 minutes and drained
16 fl. oz. [2 cups] water
½ teaspoon salt
1 tablespoon butter
2 eggs, lightly beaten
4 tablespoons vegetable oil
4 oz. French beans, cut into small pieces, blanched and drained

Ham and Fried Rice, an unusual mixture of vegetables, ham and rice cooked the Chinese way, makes a filling supper dish for family or friends.

10 oz. cooked ham, cut into very small dice
½ teaspoon black pepper
4 small spring onions [scallions]
1 tablespoon chopped fresh coriander

Put the rice, water and salt in a medium-sized saucepan. Bring the water to the boil over high heat. Cover the pan, reduce the heat to low and simmer for 15 to 20 minutes or until the rice is tender and all the water has been absorbed. Remove the pan from the heat and set aside.

In a large frying-pan, melt the butter over moderate heat. Add the eggs and cook for 2 to 3 minutes or until they are set on the underside. Stir the eggs with a fork and cook for 2 to 3 minutes more or until they are just set. Remove the pan from the heat and transfer the eggs to a small mixing bowl. Break up with the fork. Set aside.

Add the oil to the frying-pan and heat it over moderately high heat. Add the cooked rice, beans, diced ham and pepper to the pan and cook, stirring constantly, for 2 minutes or until the rice is well coated with the oil. Reduce the heat to moderate and add the spring onions [scallions] and eggs. Cook, stirring constantly, for 2 minutes or until the mixture is hot.

Remove the pan from the heat and transfer the mixture to a warmed serving dish. Sprinkle with the coriander and serve immediately.

Japanese Mixed Vegetables and Rice

Japanese Mixed Vegetables and Rice may be served as part of a Japanese meal, or with a salad for an unusual and exotic lunch, followed by a light fruit dessert. Canned ginko nuts can be bought at most oriental food stores, but if you cannot obtain them, you can omit them without spoiling the dish. Ground ginger can be substituted for the root ginger if necessary.

4 SERVINGS

1 large dried mushroom, soaked
  for 30 minutes in cold water
  and drained
2 carrots, scraped and thinly
  sliced
1-inch piece fresh root ginger,
  peeled and chopped
2 celery stalks, trimmed and
  chopped
12 canned ginko nuts, drained
2 tablespoons soy sauce
1 tablespoon sake or dry
  sherry
½ teaspoon salt
12 oz. [2 cups] long-grain rice,
  washed, soaked in cold water for
  30 minutes and drained
1¼ pints [3⅛ cups] water

4 oz. fresh peas, shelled
4 oz. cooked shrimps, shelled

Chop the mushroom finely and place it in a large saucepan. Add the carrots, ginger, celery, ginko nuts, soy sauce, sake or sherry, salt and rice.

Pour in the water, place the pan over moderate heat and bring the water to the boil. Reduce the heat to low, cover the pan and cook for 15 to 20 minutes or until the rice is tender and has absorbed most of the liquid.

Stir in the peas and shrimps and cook the mixture for a further 8 to 10 minutes or until the peas are cooked and the shrimps are heated through. If the mixture becomes too dry add a little more water.

Remove the pan from the heat and transfer the mixture to a warmed serving dish.

Serve at once.

Khichri

Khichri is a lightly aromatic mixture of rice and lentils from India and is the dish from which the English evolved Kedgeree. Serve it with spiced vegetables for a sustaining

This exotic dish from the Orient (Japanese Mixed Vegetables and Rice) includes vegetables, shrimps, rice, ginger and a Japanese speciality called ginko nuts.

meal in itself, or as a filling accompaniment to meat curries.

4 SERVINGS

2½ oz. [5 tablespoons] butter
1 medium-sized onion, finely
  chopped
1-inch piece fresh root ginger,
  peeled and very finely
  chopped
1 garlic clove, finely chopped
6 peppercorns
1 bay leaf
8 oz. [1⅓ cups] long-grain rice,
  washed, soaked in cold water for
  30 minutes and drained
4 oz. [½ cup] yellow moong dhal,
  washed, soaked in cold water for
  1 hour and drained
1 teaspoon salt
½ teaspoon turmeric
1 pint [2½ cups] boiling water
  fried onion slices to
  garnish

In a large saucepan, melt 1½ ounces [3

tablespoons] of the butter over moderate heat. When the foam subsides, add the onion and fry, stirring occasionally, for 4 minutes. Add the ginger, garlic, peppercorns and bay leaf and continue frying, stirring occasionally, for 3 minutes or until the onion is soft and translucent but not brown.

Add the rice, moong dhal, salt and turmeric. Stir and toss the mixture gently. Reduce the heat to moderately low and continue cooking and stirring gently for 5 minutes.

Pour in the boiling water and stir once. Cover the pan, reduce the heat to low and cook for 15 to 20 minutes, or until the rice and moong dhal are cooked and tender and all the water has been absorbed. With a fork, stir in the remaining butter.

Remove the pan from the heat and turn the khichri into a heated serving dish. Scatter the fried onion slices on top and serve at once.

Leftover Pork with Fried Rice

☆   ①   ⊠

This is a wonderful way to use up leftover roast pork. Serve on its own as a light luncheon dish, or for supper accompanied by a salad. Chicken or beef may be substituted for the pork if you prefer—and in similar quantities.

4 SERVINGS

3 tablespoons vegetable oil
1 medium-sized onion, finely
   chopped
2 celery stalks, trimmed and finely
   chopped
2 small carrots, scraped and finely
   chopped
8 oz. roast pork, cut into
   strips 1-inch long
½ small cabbage, coarse outer
   leaves removed, washed and
   with the leaves finely
   shredded
½ teaspoon freshly ground black
   pepper
2 tablespoons soy sauce
8 oz. [3 cups] cooked long-grain rice
2 eggs, lightly beaten
¼ teaspoon salt

In a large frying-pan, heat 2 tablespoons of the oil over moderate heat. When the oil is hot, add the onion, celery and carrots and cook, stirring constantly, for 5 minutes. Stir in the pork, cabbage, pep-per, soy sauce and rice and cook, stirring constantly, for a further 2 to 3 minutes or until the mixture is hot. Moisten with a little water or chicken stock if the mixture is dry. Set aside and keep hot while you make the garnish.

In a small frying-pan, heat the remaining oil over moderate heat. When the oil is hot, add the beaten eggs and salt and cook for 2 minutes. When the bottom is set and lightly browned turn the omelet over, using a fish slice. Cook for a further 2 to 3 minutes or until the omelet is completely set. Remove the pan from the heat and, using the fish slice, remove the omelet from the pan. Using a sharp knife, cut the omelet into strips 1-inch by ¼-inch.

Spoon the rice mixture on to a warmed serving dish. Garnish with the omelet strips.

Serve at once.

Leftover Pork with Fried Rice uses up cooked pork in this recipe, but you can substitute leftover poultry, lamb or beef if you prefer. Serve as a light but filling supper dish, with salad and a bottle of well-chilled white wine, such as Soave.

Meat and Fruit Pilaff

A festive dish of rice with lamb, fruit and nuts, Meat and Fruit Pilaff may be served as part of an Indian meal or on its own accompanied by yogurt and chutneys.

6-8 SERVINGS

2 oz. [¼ cup] butter
2 onions, sliced
1-inch piece of fresh root ginger, peeled and finely chopped
1 garlic clove, crushed
1 teaspoon ground cumin
1 tablespoon coriander seeds, crushed
1 teaspoon cardamom seeds, crushed
1 teaspoon peppercorns, crushed
1 cinnamon stick, broken in half
1 lb. boned leg of lamb, cut into ¾-inch cubes
4 oz. [⅔ cup] dried apricots
4 oz. [⅔ cup] sultanas or seedless raisins
2 oz. [½ cup] cashew nuts, slit in half
2 oz. [½ cup] slivered almonds
2 bay leaves
2 teaspoons salt
15 fl. oz. [1⅞ cups] chicken stock
3 pints [7½ cups] water
12 oz. [2 cups] basmati rice, washed, soaked in cold water for 30 minutes and drained
1½ oz. [3 tablespoons] butter, melted
½ teaspoon saffron threads soaked in 2 tablespoons boiling water for 10 minutes
2 oz. [½ cup] pistachio nuts

In a medium-sized saucepan, melt the butter over moderate heat. When the foam subsides, add the onions, ginger and garlic and fry, stirring occasionally, for 5 to 7 minutes or until the onions are soft and translucent but not brown. Add the cumin, coriander, cardamom, peppercorns and cinnamon and fry, stirring constantly, for 2 minutes.

Add the lamb cubes and fry, turning the cubes over frequently, for 10 to 15 minutes or until they are browned. Add the apricots, sultanas or raisins, cashew nuts, half the almonds, the bay leaves and 1 teaspoon of the salt. Pour in the chicken stock, cover the pan and simmer the mixture for 35 minutes or until the lamb is tender. Taste the mixture and add more salt if necessary. Remove the pan from the heat. Remove and discard the cinnamon stick. Set aside and keep warm.

Preheat the oven to moderate 350°F

Serve Meat and Fruit Pilaff with lots of yogurt, poppadums and chutney.

(Gas Mark 4, 180°C).

In a large saucepan, bring the water to the boil over high heat. Add the remaining salt and the rice and boil for 1½ minutes. Remove the pan from the heat and drain the rice in a strainer.

Pour 1 tablespoon of the melted butter into a large ovenproof casserole. Put one-third of the rice in the bottom of the casserole. Sprinkle the rice with one-third of the saffron water. With a slotted spoon, transfer half of the meat and fruit mixture to the casserole. Put in another one-third of the rice and saffron water. Add the remaining meat and fruit mixture, reserving the pan juices. Finish with a last layer of rice sprinkled with the remaining saffron water. Pour over all the reserved pan juices. Sprinkle the top with the pistachio nuts, the remaining almonds and the remaining melted butter.

Cover the casserole and put it in the oven. Bake for 20 to 30 minutes or until the rice has absorbed all the liquid.

Remove the casserole from the oven and serve the pilaff immediately.

Mee Feng Jou
PORK IN GROUND RICE

Serve Mee Feng Jou, a delicious and unusual pork dish, with a variety of dips, such as Tomato-Soy Dip (mix together equal quantities of tomato ketchup and soy sauce), Garlic-Soy Dip (finely chop 2 or 3 cloves and mix with 3 to 4 tablespoons of soy sauce) and Soy-Sherry-Chilli Dip (combine 3 tablespoons each of soy sauce and sherry with 1 tablespoon of chilli sauce).

4 SERVINGS

2 lb. leg or belly of pork
2 slices of fresh root ginger, peeled and finely chopped
2 tablespoons soy sauce
1½ teaspoons chilli sauce
5 oz. [1¼ cups] coarsely ground rice

With a sharp knife, cut the pork into 2½- by 1½-inch slices, about ¼-inch thick.

In a small bowl, mix together the ginger, soy sauce and chilli sauce. With your fingertips, rub the mixture over the pork slices to coat them evenly. Set the pork aside to marinate for 1 hour.

Heat a large dry frying-pan over moderate heat. Add the rice to the pan and cook, stirring constantly, until it begins to turn brown. Place the pork slices in the pan and turn them so that they become thickly coated with the rice.

Remove the pan from the heat.

Transfer the rice-coated pork slices to a heatproof dish. Place the dish in a

steamer, cover and steam over moderate heat for 35 to 40 minutes, or until the pork is well cooked and tender.

Remove the dish from the steamer and serve, with the dips.

Mexican Pork and Rice

Mexican Pork and Rice is a colourful and spicy dish to serve at an informal supper.

4 SERVINGS

2 tablespoons vegetable oil
1 medium-sized onion, chopped
1 lb. minced [ground] pork
8 oz. sausage meat
2 celery stalks, chopped
1 green pepper, white pith removed, seeded and cut into rings
3 oz. [½ cup] raisins
1 garlic clove, crushed
¼ teaspoon ground cumin
½ teaspoon hot chilli powder
1 tablespoon chopped fresh parsley
1 teaspoon salt
½ teaspoon black pepper
6 oz. [1 cup] long-grain rice, washed, soaked in cold water for 30 minutes and drained
14 oz. canned peeled tomatoes
4 fl. oz. [½ cup] water
2 tablespoons tomato purée
juice of ½ lemon
3 tablespoons pine nuts

Preheat the oven to moderate 350°F (Gas Mark 4, 180°C).

In a large flameproof casserole, heat the oil over moderate heat. When the oil is hot, add the onion and fry, stirring occasionally, for 5 to 7 minutes, or until it is soft and translucent but not brown. Add the pork and sausage meat and cook, stirring frequently, for 3 to 5 minutes, or until the meat is lightly browned all over.

Add the celery, green pepper, raisins, garlic, cumin, chilli powder, parsley, salt, pepper and rice. Fry the mixture, stirring constantly, for 5 to 7 minutes or until the rice has changed colour. Add the tomatoes with the can juice, the water and tomato purée and stir to mix. Simmer for 5 minutes. Reduce the heat to low, cover the casserole and cook for a further 10 minutes.

Remove the casserole from the heat and place it in the oven. Bake, covered, for 25 minutes.

Remove the casserole from the oven and sprinkle the lemon juice and the pine nuts over the top. Return the casserole to the oven, uncovered, and bake for a further 10 minutes.

Remove the casserole from the oven and serve immediately.

Risotto with Leeks and Bacon

This delightful dish is a perfect mid-week lunch or supper for the family.

4 SERVINGS

1 lb. streaky bacon slices, chopped
2 fl. oz. [¼ cup] vegetable oil
4 leeks, cleaned and chopped
1 lb. [2⅔ cups] long-grain rice, washed, soaked in cold water for 30 minutes and drained
14 oz. canned peeled tomatoes
1 teaspoon salt
1 teaspoon black pepper
½ teaspoon cayenne pepper
½ teaspoon ground cumin
1 teaspoon grated lemon rind
1½ pints [3¾ cups] chicken stock

In a flameproof casserole, fry the bacon over moderate heat for 6 to 8 minutes or until it is crisp and brown and has rendered most of its fat. Transfer the pieces to a plate and set aside.

Add the oil and heat it over moderate heat. When the oil is hot, add the leeks and fry, stirring occasionally, for 12 minutes. Stir in the rice and fry, stirring frequently, for 5 minutes. Add the tomatoes with the can juice, salt, pepper, cayenne, cumin and lemon rind and stir to mix. Pour over the stock and bring the liquid to the boil.

Return the bacon pieces to the casserole, reduce the heat to low and simmer the mixture for 15 to 20 minutes or until the rice is cooked and tender and all the liquid has been absorbed.

Remove the casserole from the heat and serve at once.

Russian Lamb Pilaff

This simple dish (pictured on page 1) may be served with a mixed salad.

4-6 SERVINGS

2 oz. [¼ cup] butter
1 tablespoon vegetable oil
2 lb. boned leg of lamb, cubed
3 onions, finely chopped
1 garlic clove, crushed
1 lb. carrots, scraped and chopped
1 lb. [2⅔ cups] long-grain rice, washed, soaked in cold water for 30 minutes and drained
1½ teaspoons dried marjoram
1½ pints [3¾ cups] strong beef stock

In a large, flameproof casserole, melt the butter with the oil over moderate heat.

Spanish Chicken with Rice.

When the foam subsides, add the lamb cubes and fry, stirring frequently, for 10 to 15 minutes or until the meat is golden brown. With a slotted spoon, transfer the meat to a plate.

Add the onions, garlic, carrots, rice and marjoram and fry, stirring constantly, for 5 to 7 minutes or until the onions are soft and translucent but not brown.

Return the meat to the casserole. Pour over the stock and bring the liquid to the boil. Reduce the heat to low, cover the casserole and simmer the mixture for 35 to 40 minutes or until the meat is tender and the liquid is absorbed.

Remove the casserole from the heat. Serve the pilaff immediately.

Spanish Chicken with Rice

This delicious chicken and rice dish is flavoured with saffron and spices.

4 SERVINGS

3 tablespoons vegetable oil
6 slices streaky bacon, chopped
1 x 5 lb. chicken, cut into serving pieces
6 tablespoons seasoned flour
2 onions, chopped
1 garlic clove, crushed
14 oz. canned peeled tomatoes
3 oz. canned pimientos, drained
2 teaspoons paprika
¼ teaspoon ground saffron
1 teaspoon salt
1 pint [2½ cups] water
8 oz. [1⅓ cups] long-grain rice, washed, soaked in cold water for 30 minutes and drained
6 oz. frozen peas, thawed

In a flameproof casserole, heat the oil over moderate heat. Add the bacon and fry until crisp. Transfer the bacon to kitchen paper towels to drain.

Coat the chicken pieces in the flour, and add to the casserole. Place over moderate heat and fry on all sides until the pieces are golden. Remove the pieces from the casserole and set aside.

Preheat the oven to moderate 350°F (Gas Mark 4, 180°C).

Drain off most of the oil from the casserole. Add the onions and garlic and fry over moderate heat for 5 minutes.

Place the chicken over the onions and add the tomatoes, with the can juice, the pimientos, paprika, saffron, salt and water. Bring to the boil. Stir in the rice.

Cover the casserole and place in the oven to cook for 35 minutes.

Add the peas and bacon and cook for a further 15 minutes or until the chicken is tender. Serve at once.

Rice Accompaniments

Coconut Rice

Coconut Rice is particularly good if made with fresh coconut. If it is not available, use creamed coconut instead.

6 SERVINGS

1 oz. [2 tablespoons] butter
1 medium-sized onion, finely chopped
1 lb [2⅔ cups] basmati rice, washed, soaked in cold water for 30 minutes and drained
1½ pints [3¾ cups] water
coconut milk made from ½ coconut, or 4 oz. slice of creamed coconut dissolved in 10 fl. oz. [1¼ cups] boiling water
1½ teaspoons salt
½ coconut

Preheat the oven to fairly hot 400°F (Gas Mark 6, 200°C).

In a saucepan, heat the butter over moderate heat. Add the onion and fry, stirring occasionally, for 5 to 7 minutes or until it is translucent but not brown.

Reduce the heat to low and add the rice. Cook, stirring constantly, for 5 minutes or until the rice is soft.

Add the water, coconut milk and salt. Increase the heat to moderately high. When the liquid is bubbling vigorously, cover the pan, reduce the heat to low and cook for 15 to 20 minutes or until the rice is tender and all the liquid absorbed.

Remove the brown outer skin of the half coconut with a sharp knife. Cut the coconut into little flakes. Spread the flaked coconut on a baking sheet lined with aluminium foil. Place the sheet in the oven and bake for 10 minutes or until the coconut turns golden brown.

When the rice is cooked, heap it on a heated serving dish. Sprinkle the top with the toasted flaked coconut and serve at once.

Hoppin' John

A traditional West Indian recipe now firmly incorporated into the American Southern 'soul' food repertoire, Hoppin' John is a spicy mixture of black-eye beans, rice, tomatoes and onion. It is particularly tasty when served with the other staples of 'soul', such as ham hocks, smothered pork chops and collard greens. Some ice-cold beer is best with this delicious but spicy food.

4-6 SERVINGS

8 oz. [1⅓ cups] dried black-eye beans, soaked in cold water overnight and drained
2 pints [5 cups] water
1½ teaspoons salt
8 oz. [1⅓ cups] long-grain rice, washed, soaked in cold water for 30 minutes and drained
1 tablespoon vegetable oil
1 medium-sized onion, finely chopped
14 oz. canned peeled tomatoes
¼ teaspoon cayenne pepper
½ teaspoon black pepper

Place the beans in a large saucepan and pour in the water and 1 teaspoon of salt. Place the pan over moderately high heat and bring to the boil. Reduce the heat to low, partially cover the pan and simmer the beans for 1½ hours.

Stir in the rice, cover the pan and simmer for 15 minutes.

Hoppin' John, a spicy soulfood dish from America, is a mixture of rice, beans, onions and tomatoes.

Meanwhile, in a small frying-pan, heat the oil over moderate heat. When the oil is hot, add the onion and cook, stirring occasionally, for 5 to 7 minutes or until the onion is soft and translucent but not brown. Remove the pan from the heat and stir in the tomatoes with the can juice, the cayenne, pepper and the remaining salt.

Pour the onion and tomato mixture into the beans and rice mixture and stir to blend the ingredients. Re-cover the pan and continue to simmer the mixture for a further 15 to 20 minutes or until the rice and beans are tender.

Remove the pan from the heat and serve at once.

Pilaff with Almonds and Mixed Fruit

This is a moist, delicately flavoured pilaff to serve with roast or fried chicken or with a vegetable casserole. Use a good quality long-grain rice such as basmati so that when the pilaff is cooked each grain remains separate.

6-8 SERVINGS

3 oz. [⅜ cup] butter
1 medium-sized onion, roughly chopped
1 large green pepper, white pith removed, seeded and roughly chopped
½ teaspoon turmeric
1 teaspoon salt
6 oz. [1 cup] dried apricots, soaked in water for 30 minutes, drained and chopped
3 oz. [½ cup] sultanas or seedless raisins
12 oz. [2 cups] long-grain rice, washed, soaked in cold water for 30 minutes and drained
1½ pints [3¾ cups] boiling chicken stock
4 oz. [1 cup] blanched flaked almonds, toasted

In a medium-sized saucepan, melt the butter over moderate heat. When the foam subsides, add the onion and green pepper and fry, stirring occasionally, for 5 to 7 minutes or until the onion is soft and translucent but not brown and the green pepper is soft.

Stir in the turmeric and salt. Add the apricots and sultanas or seedless raisins and cook, stirring constantly, for 2 minutes.

Add the rice and cook, stirring constantly, for 5 minutes. Pour in the chicken stock.

When the mixture comes to the boil,

cover the pan, reduce the heat to low and simmer the pilaff for 15 to 20 minutes or until the rice is tender and all the liquid has been absorbed. Stir in the toasted almonds.

Spoon the pilaff on to a warmed serving platter and serve immediately. Alternatively, cover the pan tightly and put it in a warm oven until you are ready to serve it.

Wild Rice with Mushrooms

A delicious dish, Wild Rice with Mushrooms may be served as a vegetable accompaniment to duck, chicken or venison. Or serve it by itself as the main course for a vegetarian meal, substituting the chicken stock with vegetable stock.

6 SERVINGS

2 oz. [¼ cup] butter
1 medium-sized onion, finely chopped
1 celery stalk, trimmed and finely chopped
8 oz. [1⅓ cups] wild rice, washed, soaked overnight and drained
6 oz. button mushrooms, wiped clean and halved
16 fl. oz. [2 cups] home-made

Wild Rice with Mushrooms is a deliciously extravagant dish—perfect for a light vegetarian meal, or as an accompaniment to roasts.

chicken stock
1 teaspoon salt
½ teaspoon freshly ground black pepper
2 oz. [½ cup] slivered almonds, toasted

In a large, heavy-based saucepan, melt the butter over moderate heat. When the foam subsides, add the onion and celery and fry, stirring occasionally, for 5 to 7 minutes or until the onion is soft and translucent but not brown.

Stir in the rice and mushrooms and fry, stirring constantly, for 3 minutes. Pour over the stock and season the mixture with the salt and pepper. Increase the heat to high and bring the liquid to the boil. Reduce the heat to low, cover the pan and simmer the mixture for 20 minutes or until the rice is tender and all the liquid has been absorbed. Remove the pan from the heat. Spoon the mixture into a warmed serving dish. Sprinkle over the toasted almonds and serve immediately.

Biryani

SPICED RICE WITH LAMB

A North Indian dish of Moghul origin, Biryani is a fragrant mixture of meat, spices, nuts and saffron rice. The traditional meat in a Biryani is lamb, but today prawns, chicken or other meats are also used by Indian cooks. It is a main dish, the quantity of lamb being double that of the rice, and so it may be served alone with a yogurt salad or as a part of a much larger and elaborate Indian meal consisting of other meat and vegetable dishes with chutneys and pickles.

6 SERVINGS

8 tablespoons butter or cooking oil
2 garlic cloves, crushed
1-inch piece fresh ginger, peeled and finely chopped
¼ teaspoon cayenne pepper
1½ teaspoons cumin seeds
2 lb. lean boned lamb, cut into 1 -inch cubes
4-inch piece of cinnamon stick
10 cloves
8 peppercorns
1 teaspoon cardamom seeds
10 fl. oz. [1¼ cups] yogurt
2 teaspoons salt
1 lb. [2⅔ cups] basmati rice, washed, soaked in cold water for 30 minutes and drained

Biryani, a combination of rice and lamb, spices and yogurt, is one of the great classics of Indian cuisine.

½ teaspoon saffron threads soaked
   in 2 tablespoons boiling water for
   10 minutes
2 onions, thinly sliced
1½ oz. [⅓ cup] almonds, slivered
1½ oz. [⅓ cup] pistachio nuts
2 oz. [⅓ cup] sultanas or raisins

In a large saucepan, heat 4 tablespoons of the butter or cooking oil over moderate heat.

Add the garlic, ginger, cayenne pepper and cumin seeds to the pan. Fry for 3 minutes. Raise the heat to moderately high, add the lamb cubes and fry for 10 to 15 minutes or until they are evenly browned. Stir in the cinnamon, cloves, peppercorns, cardamom, yogurt and 1 teaspoon of salt. Mix well and add 5 fluid ounces [⅝ cup] of water. Bring the mixture to the boil. Reduce the heat to low, cover the pan and simmer for 40 minutes or until the lamb is tender.

In a second saucepan, bring 3 pints of water to the boil over moderate heat. Add the remaining salt and pour in the rice. Boil briskly for 1½ minutes. Remove the pan from the heat, drain the rice thoroughly and set aside.

Preheat the oven to moderate 350°F (Gas Mark 4, 180°C).

Pour 1 tablespoon of butter or oil into a large ovenproof casserole dish. Put one-third of the parboiled rice in the bottom of the casserole. Sprinkle one-third of the saffron water over it. With a slotted spoon, remove one-third of the lamb cubes from the saucepan and put them over the rice. Cover with another one-third of the rice sprinkled with saffron water. Remove all the remaining meat cubes from the pan with the slotted spoon and put them on top, then finish with a last layer of the remaining rice. Pour all the liquid left in the saucepan in which the lamb was cooked carefully over the rice and meat. Sprinkle the remaining saffron water over the top layer of rice.

Cover the casserole with aluminium foil. Place the casserole in the oven and cook for 20 to 30 minutes or until the rice is cooked and has absorbed all the liquid.

In a small frying-pan, heat the remaining butter or oil over high heat. Add the onions, reduce the heat to moderate and, stirring frequently, fry for 8 to 10 minutes or until they are golden brown. With a slotted spoon, remove the onions and set aside on kitchen paper towels to drain.

Add the almonds, pistachio nuts and sultanas or raisins to the pan, adding more butter or oil if necessary. Fry them for 3 minutes or until the nuts are lightly browned. With a slotted spoon, remove

the mixture from the pan and set aside on a plate.

Pile the rice and lamb attractively on a large heated serving dish and sprinkle the top with the nuts, sultanas and onions. Serve immediately.

Gamberi con Riso

A delicious rice dish from Italy, Gamberi con Riso may be eaten on its own with only a green salad to follow. Serve it with a well-chilled Toscano Bianco. Italian rice, unlike basmati or patna, needs no washing or soaking.

4 SERVINGS

2 oz. [¼ cup] butter
2 tablespoons olive oil
1 large onion, finely chopped
1 garlic clove, finely chopped
1 medium-sized red pepper, white
   pith removed, seeded and chopped
4 oz. button mushrooms, wiped
   clean and chopped
½ teaspoon dried basil
1 teaspoon salt
½ teaspoon black pepper
12 oz. [2 cups] Italian rice, such as
   avorio
12 oz. frozen shrimps, thawed and
   shelled
1½ pints [3¾ cups] boiling water

2 oz. [½ cup] Parmesan cheeese,
   grated

In a large, heavy frying-pan, melt half the butter with the oil over moderately high heat. When the foam subsides, reduce the heat to moderate. Add the onion, garlic and pepper and fry them, stirring occasionally, for 5 to 7 minutes, or until the onion is soft and translucent but not brown. Stir in the mushrooms, basil, salt and pepper. Cook, stirring occasionally, for 5 minutes.

Add the rice, reduce the heat to low, and cook, stirring frequently, for 5 minutes. Stir in the shrimps and cook for 1 minute. Add approximately one-third of the boiling water. Regulate the heat so that the rice is bubbling all the time. Stir the rice occasionally with a fork. When the rice swells and the liquid is absorbed, add another one-third of the water. Continue cooking the rice in this way until the rice is tender and moist but still firm.

Remove the pan from the heat and stir in the remaining butter and the cheese. Turn the mixture into a warmed serving dish and serve at once.

Gamberi con Riso is a succulent Italian mixture of rice, shrimps, vegetables and Parmesan cheese.

Jambalaya

One of the most popular Creole dishes from the southern United States, Jambalaya is a delicious dinner party dish. Serve with crusty bread and a tossed green salad and, to drink, some well-chilled white wine, such as Californian Chablis.

4-6 SERVINGS

1 tablespoon vegetable oil
3 lean bacon slices, rinds removed and chopped
1 medium-sized onion, finely chopped
2 celery stalks, trimmed and chopped
12 oz. [2 cups] long-grain rice, washed, soaked in cold water for 30 minutes and drained
1 pint [2½ cups] chicken stock
½ teaspoon salt
½ teaspoon freshly ground black pepper
⅛ teaspoon cayenne pepper
1 bay leaf
1 large green pepper, white pith removed, seeded and roughly chopped
14 oz. canned peeled tomatoes
4 oz. cooked ham
8 oz. cooked shrimps, shelled
8 oz. cooked chicken meat, chopped
1 tablespoon finely chopped fresh parsley

Jambalya, a fabulous mixture of rice, vegetables, meat and shrimps, comes from the southern part of the United States.

In a large saucepan, heat the oil over moderate heat. When the oil is hot, add the bacon and fry, stirring occasionally, for 6 minutes or until it is crisp and golden brown. With a slotted spoon, remove the bacon from the pan and drain on kitchen paper towels. Set the bacon aside.

Add the onion to the frying-pan and cook, stirring occasionally, for 8 to 10 minutes or until it is golden brown. Add the celery, then stir in the rice. Cook, stirring constantly, for 3 minutes or until the rice is well coated with the fat. Pour in the chicken stock, stirring constantly. Add the salt, pepper, cayenne and bay leaf. Reduce the heat to low, cover the pan and simmer the mixture for 10 minutes.

Add the green pepper and tomatoes with the can juice and simmer, covered, for a further 5 minutes.

Add the ham, shrimps, chicken and reserved bacon pieces and stir well. Re-cover the pan and cook the mixture for a further 5 minutes or until the meats and shrimps are heated through and the rice is tender.

Remove the pan from the heat and transfer the mixture to a warmed serving dish. Sprinkle over the parsley and serve at once.

Kedgeree of Salmon

Kedgeree of Salmon is a richer version of plain kedgeree and makes an excellent family supper or a festive meal for unexpected guests. Accompany with a colourful tossed mixed salad and lots of generously buttered toast.

4 SERVINGS

1¼ lb. canned salmon, drained and flaked
10 fl. oz. double cream [1¼ cups heavy cream], beaten until thick but not stiff
½ teaspoon grated nutmeg
2 oz. [¼ cup] butter
1 medium-sized onion, finely chopped
10 oz. [4 cups] cooked long-grain rice
2 hard-boiled eggs, finely chopped
½ teaspoon salt
¼ teaspoon freshly ground black pepper
2 teaspoons curry powder

In a medium-sized saucepan, combine the salmon, cream and nutmeg together, stirring to mix. Set the pan over moderate heat and cook the mixture, stirring occasionally, for 3 to 5 minutes, or until the fish is heated through. Remove the pan from the heat.

In a large saucepan, melt the butter over moderate heat. When the foam subsides, add the onion and cook, stirring occasionally, for 5 to 7 minutes, or until it is soft and translucent but not brown. Stir in the cooked rice and half of the chopped eggs, then stir in the salmon mixture, the salt, black pepper and curry powder.

Remove the pan from the heat and pile the mixture on to a large warmed serving dish. Sprinkle over the remaining chopped egg.

Serve immediately.

Lamb and Mixed Fruit Pilaff

An exotic and satisfying dish, Lamb and Mixed Fruit Pilaff makes a delicious dinner party centrepiece. Serve with a tossed green salad, some crusty bread and a well-chilled bottle of Greek white wine, such as Hymettus or Retsina.

4 SERVINGS

4 oz. [½ cup] butter
1 medium-sized onion, thinly sliced
1½ lb. boned leg of lamb, cut into 1-inch cubes
3 oz. [½ cup] dried apricots, soaked overnight in cold water, drained and halved
3 tablespoons sultanas or seedless raisins
2 teaspoons salt
½ teaspoon ground cinnamon
¼ teaspoon freshly ground black pepper
1½ pints [3¾ cups] water
8 oz. [1⅓ cups] long-grain rice, washed, soaked in cold water for 30 minutes and drained

In a large, deep frying-pan, melt the butter over moderate heat. When the foam subsides, add the onion and cook, stirring occasionally, for 5 to 7 minutes, or until it is soft and translucent but not brown.

Add the lamb and cook, stirring and turning occasionally, for 5 to 8 minutes, or until it is lightly browned all over. Stir in the apricots, sultanas or seedless raisins, 1 teaspoon of the salt, the cinnamon and pepper.

Pour in 16 fluid ounces [2 cups] of the water and bring to the boil, stirring occasionally. Reduce the heat to moderately low, cover the pan and simmer the meat for 1 hour, or until the meat is tender when pierced with the point of a sharp knife.

Meanwhile, put the rice in a medium-sized saucepan. Pour over the remaining water and add the remaining salt. Place the saucepan over high heat and bring the water to the boil. Reduce the heat to low, cover the pan and simmer the rice for 15 to 20 minutes. If all the liquid is not absorbed, continue to cook the rice, uncovered, over low heat until the rice is dry. Remove the saucepan from the heat and set aside.

Preheat the oven to moderate 350°F (Gas Mark 4, 180°C). Place one-third of the rice in a medium-sized ovenproof casserole. Cover with a layer of one-half of the meat mixture, then top with another one-third of the rice. Continue to make layers in this manner until all the ingredients have been used up, finishing with a layer of rice. Cover the casserole with a lid and carefully place it in the centre of the oven. Bake the pilaff for 20 minutes.

Remove the casserole from the oven and serve the pilaff at once, straight from the casserole.

A rice dish from the Balkans, Lamb and Mixed Fruit Pilaff makes a superb and relatively inexpensive main course for a family supper or informal entertaining. Serve with some well-chilled white wine.

Liver and Rice

This delicious dish is traditionally Indonesian and makes a festive main course.

6-8 SERVINGS

- 1 lb. [2⅔ cups] long-grain rice, washed, soaked in cold water for 30 minutes and drained
- 2 pints [5 cups] water
- 1 teaspoon salt
- 3 tablespoons peanut oil
- 3 eggs, lightly beaten
- 4 spring onions [scallions], trimmed and chopped
- 3 oz. button mushrooms, wiped clean and sliced
- 1 red chilli, finely chopped
- 2 garlic cloves, crushed

2-inch piece fresh root ginger, peeled and very finely chopped
2 tablespoons soy sauce

LIVER
- 4 tablespoons soy sauce
- 4 tablespoons beef stock
- 1 tablespoon wine vinegar
- 2 tablespoons water
- 1 teaspoon black pepper
- 4-inch piece fresh root ginger, peeled and very finely chopped
- 2 teaspoons cornflour [cornstarch]
- 3 lb. lamb's liver, thinly sliced
- 2 fl. oz. [¼ cup] peanut oil
- 2 celery stalks, finely chopped
- 12 oz. bean sprouts

First prepare the liver. In a large, shallow dish, combine the soy sauce, beef stock,

Liver and Rice is a Dutch adaptation of a traditional Indonesian dish called Nasi Goreng.

vinegar, water, pepper, half of the ginger and the cornflour [cornstarch]. Place the liver slices in the mixture and baste well. Set aside to marinate for 45 minutes, basting frequently.

Meanwhile, prepare the rice. Put the rice in a large saucepan. Pour over the water and add the salt. Bring the water to the boil over high heat. Cover the pan, reduce the heat to low and simmer for 15 to 20 minutes or until the rice is tender and has absorbed all the liquid. Remove the pan from the heat.

In a small frying-pan, heat 1 tablespoon

22

of the oil over moderate heat. When the oil is hot, add the eggs and fry for 3 minutes on each side or until they are set in a thin omelet. Remove the pan from the heat. Cut the omelet into thin strips about 2-inches long and ½-inch wide.

Preheat the oven to very cool 250°F (Gas Mark ½, 130°C).

In a large frying-pan, heat the remaining oil over moderate heat. When the oil is hot, add the spring onions [scallions], mushrooms, chilli, garlic and ginger and fry, stirring occasionally, for 3 to 4 minutes or until the spring onions [scallions] are soft and translucent but not brown. Stir in the cooked rice, soy sauce and omelet strips and fry, stirring occasionally, for 3 minutes or until all the ingredients are warmed through.

Transfer the mixture to a warmed, ovenproof serving dish. Place in the oven and keep hot while you cook the liver.

In a large frying-pan, heat the oil over moderate heat. When the oil is hot, add the remaining ginger and fry, stirring constantly, for 2 minutes. Increase the heat to moderately high and add the liver slices and marinade to the pan. Fry, stirring and turning occasionally, for 6 minutes. Stir in the celery and bean sprouts and continue to fry, stirring and turning occasionally, for a further 3 minutes or until the liver is cooked.

Remove the serving dish from the oven and arrange the liver slices decoratively over the rice. Spoon over the sauce and vegetables and serve at once.

Morue à l'Americaine
SALT COD WITH RICE AND BRANDY AND WINE SAUCE

Salt cod is a relatively exotic delicacy in the English-speaking world, but around the Mediterranean it is consumed with great relish. The recipe below for Morue à l'Americaine is easy to prepare — and makes a deliciously different dinner dish.

4 SERVINGS

10 oz. [1⅔ cups] long-grain rice, washed, soaked in cold water for 30 minutes and drained
1 pint [2½ cups] water
1½ teaspoons salt
2 lb. salt cod, soaked in cold water for 24 hours
3 tablespoons olive oil
1 large onion, finely chopped
1 garlic clove, crushed
5 oz. canned tomato purée
½ teaspoon black pepper
8 fl. oz. [1 cup] dry white wine
2 fl. oz. [¼ cup] brandy
1 oz. [2 tablespoons] butter

Put the rice in a saucepan. Pour over the water and add 1 teaspoon of the salt. Place the pan over moderate heat and bring the water to the boil. Cover the pan, reduce the heat to low and simmer the rice for 15 to 20 minutes, or until all the liquid has been absorbed and the rice is tender. Remove the pan from the heat.

Drain the salt cod and dry it on kitchen paper towels. Skin the cod and chop into 1½-inch pieces. Set aside.

In a large frying-pan, heat the oil over moderate heat. When the oil is hot, add the onion and garlic and cook, stirring occasionally, for 5 to 7 minutes, or until the onion is soft and translucent but not brown. Stir in the tomato purée, the remaining salt and the pepper and cook, stirring occasionally, for 3 minutes. Stir in the wine and bring the mixture to the boil, stirring frequently.

Add the salt cod and brandy to the pan, stirring to combine. Reduce the heat to low, cover the pan and cook, stirring and turning from time to time, for 15 to 20 minutes, or until the fish flakes easily.

Meanwhile, in a saucepan, melt the butter over moderate heat. When the foam subsides, add the rice to the pan. Cook, stirring frequently, for 3 to 5 minutes, or until the rice is heated through and is coated with the butter.

Remove the pan from the heat. Arrange the rice in a ring on a warmed serving platter. Remove the frying-pan from the heat, spoon the fish and sauce into the centre and serve.

Morue à l'Americaine is a popular French dish of salt cod and rice.

Paella
SPANISH RICE WITH CHICKEN AND SEAFOOD

☆ ① ① ① ✕ ✕

Traditionally, Paella is made from a combination of chicken, seafood, sausage, vegetables and rice. It can vary from a simple supper dish made with a few inexpensive chicken pieces and a handful of shrimps to an elaborate party dish with lobster and mussels.

4-6 SERVINGS

1 x 1½ lb. cooked lobster, shell split, claws cracked and grey sac removed
2 tablespoons olive oil
1 x 2 lb. chicken, cut into 8 serving pieces
1 chorizo sausage, sliced
1 onion, thinly sliced
1 garlic clove, crushed
3 tomatoes, blanched, peeled, seeded and chopped or 8 oz. canned peeled tomatoes, drained
1 large red pepper, white pith removed, seeded and chopped
1 teaspoon salt
½ teaspoon black pepper
1 teaspoon paprika
12 oz. [2 cups] long-grain rice, washed, soaked in cold water for 30 minutes and drained
1 pint [2½ cups] water
juice of 1 lemon
⅛ teaspoon ground saffron, soaked in 4 fl. oz. [½ cup] hot water for 20 minutes
8 oz. fresh peas, shelled
6 oz. large prawns or shrimps, shelled
1 quart mussels, scrubbed, steamed and removed from their shells
1 tablespoon chopped fresh parsley

Remove the lobster meat from the shell and claws and cut it into 1-inch pieces.

In a large flameproof casserole, heat the olive oil over moderate heat. When it is hot, add the chicken pieces and chorizo sausage slices and fry, turning occasionally, for 10 to 15 minutes or until the chicken is evenly browned.

Using tongs or a slotted spoon, remove the chicken pieces and sausage slices from the pan. Set aside and keep hot.

Add the onion and garlic to the casserole and fry, stirring occasionally, for 5 to 7 minutes or until the onion is soft and translucent but not brown. Add the tomatoes, red pepper, salt, pepper and paprika and cook, stirring occasionally, for 10 to 12 minutes or until the mixture

The Spanish national dish—Paella.

is thick and pulpy.

Add the rice and, shaking the casserole frequently, fry it for 3 minutes or until it is transparent. Add the water, lemon juice and saffron, and bring to the boil. Reduce the heat to low and stir in the peas. Return the chicken pieces and sausage slices to the pan and cook for 15 minutes, stirring occasionally. Add the lobster, prawns or shrimps and mussels and cook for a further 5 minutes or until the chicken is cooked and the cooking liquid has been absorbed.

Remove from the heat. Sprinkle over the parsley and serve immediately.

Picardy Rice

☆ ① ✕

Picardy Rice, a tasty mixture of rice, chicken, tomatoes, bacon and vegetables, may be served as a meal in itself.

4-6 SERVINGS

4 streaky bacon slices, diced
1 oz. [2 tablespoons] butter
2 shallots, finely chopped
2 small green peppers, white pith removed, seeded and cut into julienne strips
2 medium-sized tomatoes, blanched, peeled and chopped
1 teaspoon salt
½ teaspoon black pepper
½ teaspoon dried thyme
12 oz. [2 cups] long-grain rice, washed, soaked in cold water for 30 minutes and drained
1 pint [2½ cups] hot chicken stock
1 lb. lean cooked chicken, cut into strips

In a flameproof casserole, fry the bacon over moderate heat for 5 minutes or until it is crisp and has rendered most of its fat. Scrape the bottom of the casserole frequently with a wooden spoon to prevent the bacon from sticking.

With a slotted spoon, remove the bacon from the casserole and drain it on kitchen paper towels. Set aside.

Add the butter to the casserole. When the foam subsides, add the shallots and green peppers and fry, stirring frequently, for 3 to 4 minutes or until the shallots are soft and translucent but not brown. Stir in the tomatoes, salt, pepper and thyme. Add the rice and stir well to coat the grains. Pour in the stock and bring to the boil, stirring occasionally.

Reduce the heat to low and simmer stirring occasionally, for 15 to 20 minutes. Stir in the chicken and simmer for a further 5 minutes, or until the rice is cooked and tender and has absorbed the cooking liquid.

Remove the casserole from the heat and spoon the rice mixture into a large warmed serving dish. Sprinkle over the fried bacon and serve immediately.

Pilaff à la Grecque
RICE COOKED WITH MUSHROOMS

☆ ①

Use a good quality long-grain rice for this dish to ensure that the grains of rice remain separate when cooked. Pilaff à la Grecque may be served by itself or with kebabs.

4-6 SERVINGS

2 oz. [¼ cup] plus 1 tablespoon butter
1 onion, finely chopped
2 garlic cloves, crushed
12 oz. [2 cups] long-grain rice, washed, soaked in cold water for 30 minutes and drained
8 oz. button mushrooms, wiped clean
1 teaspoon salt
½ teaspoon black pepper
1½ pints [3¾ cups] hot chicken stock
1 bay leaf
thinly pared rind of 1 lemon, in one piece
GARNISH
2 tablespoons slivered almonds
2 tablespoons raisins
8 large black olives, stoned

In a saucepan, melt 2 ounces [¼ cup] of the butter over moderate heat. When the foam subsides, add the onion and garlic and fry for 5 to 7 minutes or until the onion is soft and translucent but not brown. Add the rice and cook, stirring constantly, for 5 minutes. Add the mushrooms, and cook, stirring constantly, for 3 minutes.

Stir in the salt and pepper and pour in the stock.

Increase the heat to high and add the bay leaf and lemon rind. When the stock is boiling vigorously, cover the pan, reduce the heat to low and simmer for 15 to 20 minutes or until the rice is tender and all the liquid has been absorbed.

Meanwhile, in a small frying-pan, melt the remaining butter over moderate heat. When the foam subsides, add the almonds and raisins and fry them, stirring constantly, for 5 minutes or until the almonds are browned and the raisins puffed up.

Remove the pan from the heat.

Remove the pilaff from the heat. Remove and discard the bay leaf and the lemon rind. Spoon the pilaff on to a warmed serving platter and scatter the almonds, raisins and the olives over the top. Serve immediately.

Pilaff with Pineapple and Cashew Nuts

A subtle mixture of taste and texture makes this pilaff an exciting accompaniment to roast lamb. Or serve it on its own, accompanied by a green salad.

4 SERVINGS

3 oz. [⅜ cup] butter
1 small pineapple, peeled, cored and cut into chunks
3 tablespoons raisins
12 spring onions [scallions], chopped
2½ oz. [½ cup] cashew nuts
1 tablespoon coriander seeds, coarsely crushed
¼ teaspoon cayenne pepper
12 oz. [2 cups] long-grain rice, washed, soaked in cold water for 30 minutes and drained
1 teaspoon salt
1 pint [2½ cups] chicken stock
2 hard-boiled eggs, quartered
1 tablespoon chopped coriander leaves

In a frying-pan, melt half of the butter over moderate heat. When the foam subsides, add the pineapple chunks and raisins and fry, turning them frequently, for 2 to 3 minutes or until the pineapple is lightly coloured. Remove the pan from the heat and set aside.

In a large saucepan, melt the remaining butter over moderate heat. When the foam subsides, add the spring onions [scallions] and fry them, stirring occasionally, for 4 to 6 minutes or until they are golden brown.

Add the cashew nuts, coriander seeds and cayenne and fry, stirring occasionally, for 4 minutes.

Add the rice and the salt and fry, stirring constantly, for 5 minutes. Stir in the pineapple mixture. Pour in the chicken stock and bring the mixture to the boil.

Cover the pan, reduce the heat to low and cook the pilaff for 15 to 20 minutes or until the rice is tender and all the liquid has been absorbed.

Pilaff with Pineapple and Cashew Nuts is a delicate rice dish from India. Serve on its own or with meat.

Taste the pilaff and add more salt and pepper if necessary.

Remove the pan from the heat and spoon the pilaff on to a warmed serving platter. Garnish with the hard-boiled eggs and the chopped coriander leaves.

Serve immediately.

Rice with Shellfish

Serve this sustaining dish with a tossed green salad and a well-chilled dry white wine, such as Muscadet.

4 SERVINGS

2 oz. [¼ cup] butter
8 oz. [1⅓ cups] long-grain rice, washed, soaked in cold water for 30 minutes and drained
8 fl. oz. [1 cup] fish stock
10 fl. oz. [1¼ cups] water
1½ teaspoons salt
1 teaspoon black pepper
3 large tomatoes, blanched, peeled, seeded and chopped
2 garlic cloves, crushed
1 tablespoon flour

2 quarts mussels, scrubbed,
  steamed, removed from their
  shells and 4 fl. oz. [½ cup] of the
  cooking fluid reserved
8 fl. oz. [1 cup] dry white wine
1 tablespoon lemon juice
1 tablespoon sweet vermouth
1 lb. scallops, scrubbed and
  removed from their shells
8 oz. frozen Dublin Bay prawns
  [large Gulf shrimps], thawed
4 oz. [1 cup] Parmesan cheese,
  grated

In a large saucepan, melt 1 ounce [2
tablespoons] of the butter over moderate
heat. When the foam subsides, add the
rice and fry, stirring constantly, for 3
minutes. Pour over the stock and water
and add half the salt and pepper, the
tomatoes and garlic. Bring the liquid to
the boil, stirring constantly. Reduce the
heat to low, cover tightly and simmer for
20 minutes or until the rice is cooked and
tender and has absorbed all the liquid.

Meanwhile, in a medium-sized saucepan, melt the remaining butter over
moderate heat. Remove the pan from the
heat. Stir in the flour and the remaining
salt and pepper with a wooden spoon to
make a smooth paste. Gradually add the
reserved mussel liquid, the wine, lemon
juice and vermouth, stirring constantly
and being careful to avoid lumps.

*Rice with Shellfish is rice, mussels,
scallops and prawns or shrimps in
a creamy white wine sauce.*

Return the pan to the heat and cook
the sauce, stirring constantly, for 3
minutes or until it is smooth and has
thickened slightly. Remove from the
heat and spoon half the sauce into a
warmed sauceboat. Set aside and keep
warm.

Return the pan to the heat and add the
mussels, scallops and prawns [shrimps].
Cook the shellfish, stirring frequently, for
5 minutes. Remove the pan from the heat
and keep warm.

Remove the rice from the heat and stir
in half the grated cheese. Spoon the rice
mixture into a warmed serving dish and
spoon over the fish mixture. Place the
remaining cheese in a small serving bowl
and serve immediately, with the sauce.

Spanish Rice

*Spanish Rice may be served with crusty
bread and a mixed salad, as a light luncheon
dish.*

3-4 SERVINGS

3 tablespoons olive oil
2 onions, thinly sliced

1 garlic clove, crushed
1 green pepper, white pith
  removed, seeded and thinly sliced
2 red peppers, white pith removed,
  seeded and thinly sliced
12 oz. mushrooms, wiped clean and
  sliced
14 oz. canned peeled tomatoes,
  chopped
1½ oz. [⅓ cup] stoned green olives
1 teaspoon dried oregano
½ teaspoon dried basil
½ teaspoon salt
¼ teaspoon black pepper
5 oz. [2 cups] cooked rice

In a large frying-pan, heat the oil over
moderate heat. When the oil is hot, add
the onions and garlic to the pan and cook,
stirring occasionally, for 5 to 7 minutes
or until the onions are soft and translucent
but not brown.

Add the green and red peppers and
cook for 4 minutes, stirring frequently.
Add the mushrooms, tomatoes with the
can juice, olives, oregano, basil, salt and
pepper to the pan and cook, stirring
occasionally, for 3 minutes.

Add the rice to the pan and cook for 3
to 4 minutes, stirring constantly, or until
the rice is heated through.

Transfer the mixture to a warmed
serving dish. Serve immediately, if you
are serving it hot.

Risi e Bisi
RICE WITH PEAS

A classic Venetian dish, Risi e Bisi is a delicious combination of rice, peas and bacon. Serve Risi e Bisi as a deliciously different first course to an Italian meal or, with lots of crusty bread and mixed salad, for a sustaining lunch or supper. A well-chilled Frascati wine would complement this dish.

4-6 SERVINGS

1 tablespoon olive oil
6 oz. lean bacon, chopped
2 oz. [¼ cup] butter
1 onion, thinly sliced
1 lb. peas, weighed after shelling
1 lb. [2⅔ cups] Italian rice, such as avorio
3 fl. oz. [⅜ cup] dry white wine
2 pints [5 cups] boiling chicken stock
1 teaspoon salt
½ teaspoon black pepper
4 oz. [1 cup] Parmesan cheese, grated

In a large, heavy saucepan, heat the oil over moderate heat. When the oil is hot, add the bacon and fry, stirring occasionally, for 5 minutes or until it is crisp and golden brown. With a slotted spoon, transfer the bacon to kitchen paper towels to drain.

Add 1 ounce [2 tablespoons] of butter to the pan and melt it over moderate heat. When the foam subsides, add the onion and cook, stirring occasionally, for 5 to 7 minutes or until the onion is soft and translucent but not brown.

Add the peas and rice to the pan, reduce the heat to low and cook, stirring frequently, for 5 minutes. Pour over the wine and approximately one-third of the boiling stock. Regulate the heat so that the rice is bubbling all the time. Stir the rice occasionally with a fork. When the rice swells and the liquid is absorbed add another one-third of the stock. Continue cooking the rice in this way until it is tender and moist but still firm.

Stir in the bacon, the remaining butter, the salt, pepper and grated cheese and mix well to blend. Simmer for 1 minute, stirring frequently.

Remove the pan from the heat and transfer the risotto to a warmed serving bowl. Serve at once.

Risotto alla Bolognese
BRAISED RICE WITH HAM AND
BOLOGNESE SAUCE

This light dish is a mixture of Italian rice, Parma ham, meat sauce and grated cheese. *Serve as a light lunch or supper with garlic bread and a mixed salad.*

4-6 SERVINGS

4 oz. [½ cup] butter
1 medium-sized onion, thinly sliced
4 oz. Parma ham, chopped
1 lb. [2⅔ cups] Italian rice, such as avorio
3 fl. oz. [⅜ cup] dry white wine
2 pints [5 cups] boiling beef stock
1 oz. [¼ cup] Parmesan cheese, grated

BOLOGNESE SAUCE
1 oz. [2 tablespoons] butter
2 oz. lean ham, chopped
1 small onion, chopped
½ carrot, scraped and chopped
1 celery stalk, trimmed and chopped
4 oz. lean minced [ground] beef
2 oz. chicken livers, chopped
8 oz. canned peeled tomatoes, drained
2 tablespoons tomato purée
3 fl. oz. [⅜ cup] dry white wine
6 fl. oz. [¾ cup] chicken stock
½ teaspoon dried basil
½ teaspoon salt
¼ teaspoon black pepper

First make the sauce. In a large saucepan, melt the butter over moderate heat. When the foam subsides, add the ham, onion, carrot and celery. Cook, stirring occasionally, for 8 to 10 minutes or until the onion is golden brown. Add the beef to the pan and cook, stirring occasionally, for 10 minutes or until it is well browned.

Add all the remaining ingredients and stir well to mix. Reduce the heat to low, cover and simmer the mixture for about 1 hour.

Meanwhile, make the rice. In a large saucepan, melt 3 ounces [⅜ cup] of the butter over moderate heat. When the foam subsides, add the onion and cook, stirring occasionally, for 5 to 7 minutes or until it is soft and translucent but not brown.

Add the ham and rice, reduce the heat to low and cook, stirring frequently, for 5 minutes. Pour over the wine and approximately one-third of the boiling stock. Regulate the heat so that the rice is bubbling all the time. Stir the rice occasionally with a fork. When the rice

Three of the glories of Italian cuisine (from left to right) Risotto con Funghi (rice with mushrooms), Risi e Bisi (rice with peas) and Risotto alla Bolognese (rice with ham and bolognese sauce). Serve them as filling first courses.

swells and the liquid is absorbed, add another one-third of the stock. Continue cooking the rice in this way until it is tender and moist but still firm.

Stir in the remaining butter, the bolognese sauce and grated cheese and mix well to blend. Simmer for 1 minute, stirring frequently.

Remove the pan from the heat and transfer the risotto to a warmed serving bowl. Serve at once.

Risotto con Funghi
BRAISED RICE WITH MUSHROOMS

A light, attractive dish, Risotto con Funghi is a mixture of Italian rice, mushrooms, onion and grated cheese. It may be served with garlic bread and a mixed salad as a light lunch or supper.

4-6 SERVINGS

- 3 oz. [⅜ cup] butter
- 1 medium-sized onion, finely chopped
- 1 garlic clove, crushed
- 1 lb. [2⅔ cups] Italian rice, such as avorio
- 3 fl. oz. [⅜ cup] dry white wine
- 2 pints [5 cups] boiling beef stock
- 10 oz. mushrooms, wiped clean and sliced
- ½ teaspoon grated nutmeg
- ⅛ teaspoon cayenne pepper
- ½ teaspoon salt
- ¼ teaspoon black pepper
- 2 oz. [½ cup] Parmesan cheese, grated

In a large, heavy saucepan, melt 2 ounces [¼ cup] of the butter over moderate heat. When the foam subsides, add the onion and garlic and cook, stirring occasionally, for 5 to 7 minutes or until the onion is soft and translucent but not brown.

Add the rice to the pan, reduce the heat to low and cook, stirring frequently, for 5 minutes. Pour over the wine and approximately one-third of the boiling stock. Regulate the heat so that the liquid is bubbling all the time. Stir the rice occasionally with a fork. When the rice swells and the liquid is absorbed add another one-third of the stock. Continue cooking the rice in this way until it is tender and moist but still firm.

Stir in the mushrooms, nutmeg, cayenne, salt and pepper and cook, stirring occasionally, for 3 minutes. Stir in the remaining butter and the grated cheese and mix well to blend. Simmer for 1 minute, stirring frequently.

Remove the pan from the heat and transfer the risotto to a warmed serving bowl. Serve at once.

Rizotto Corine

RICE WITH CHICKEN AND VEGETABLES

A hearty, nourishing rice dish from Belgium, Rizotto Corine is a complete meal served with brown bread and butter.

4-6 SERVINGS

- 6 streaky bacon slices, diced
- 2 oz. [¼ cup] butter
- 2 chicken breasts, skinned, boned and cut into strips
- 2 medium-sized onions, thinly sliced and pushed out into rings
- 2 large green peppers, white pith removed, seeded and coarsely chopped
- 8 oz. small button mushrooms, wiped clean and halved
- 10 oz. [1⅔ cups] long-grain rice, washed, soaked in cold water for 30 minutes and drained
- 5 medium-sized tomatoes, blanched, peeled and chopped
- 10 oz. canned sweetcorn, drained
- ½ teaspoon dried thyme
- 1 teaspoon salt
- ½ teaspoon black pepper
- ¼ teaspoon celery salt
- ¼ teaspoon cayenne pepper
- 2 teaspoons Worcestershire sauce (optional)
- 15 fl. oz. [1⅞ cups] chicken stock
- 2 oz. [½ cup] Parmesan cheese, grated

In a medium-sized flameproof casserole, fry the bacon over moderate heat for 5 minutes or until it is crisp and golden and has rendered most of its fat. Scrape the bottom of the pan frequently with a spatula to prevent the bacon from sticking.

Using a slotted spoon, remove the bacon from the casserole and drain it on kitchen paper towels. Set aside on a large plate.

Add half of the butter to the casserole. When the foam subsides, add the chicken strips and fry them, stirring frequently, for 6 to 8 minutes or until the chicken is lightly browned.

Using the slotted spoon, remove the chicken from the casserole and set it aside with the bacon.

Add the onions and peppers to the casserole and fry, stirring frequently, for 5 minutes. Add the mushrooms and fry, stirring frequently, for a further 3 minutes.

Using the slotted spoon, remove the vegetables from the casserole and set them aside with the chicken.

Add the remaining butter to the casserole and, when the foam subsides, add the rice. Fry, stirring constantly, for 3 minutes. Stir in the chicken, bacon and vegetables, the tomatoes, sweetcorn, thyme, salt, pepper, celery salt, cayenne and the Worcestershire sauce, if you are using it. Stir well to mix and pour over the stock.

Bring the liquid to the boil, stirring constantly. Reduce the heat to very low, cover the pan and simmer for 20 minutes, or until the rice is cooked and tender and has absorbed all the liquid.

Remove the casserole from the heat. Transfer to a serving dish, sprinkle over the Parmesan and serve.

Chicken, mixed vegetables and rice form the basis of this delicious dish from Belgium, Rizotto Corine. Serve as a sustaining lunch or dinner, accompanied by a mixed salad.

Wild Rice Casserole

 ① ① ⧗

A really delicious, if somewhat extravagant dish, Wild Rice Casserole is super served with a crisp green salad.

6 SERVINGS

2 oz. [¼ cup] butter
1 large onion, finely chopped
1 garlic clove, crushed
1½ lb. boned cooked chicken, cut into ½-inch cubes
8 oz. button mushrooms, wiped clean and sliced
1 teaspoon dried thyme
1 teaspoon salt
½ teaspoon black pepper
1 teaspoon mushroom ketchup
8 oz. [1⅓ cups] wild rice, washed, soaked overnight and drained
16 fl. oz. [2 cups] chicken stock
8 oz. [2 cups] Cheddar cheese, grated

Preheat the oven to moderate 350°F (Gas Mark 4, 180°C).

In a flameproof casserole, melt the butter over moderate heat. When the foam subsides, add the onion and garlic and fry, stirring constantly, for 5 to 7 minutes or until the onion is soft and translucent but not brown. Add the chicken, mushrooms, thyme, salt, pepper and ketchup. Stir in the rice and pour over the stock. Increase the heat to high

A fabulous, informal dish—Wild Rice Meat Loaf with Barbecue Sauce.

and bring the liquid to the boil.

Cover the casserole and transfer it to the oven. Cook the mixture for 20 to 25 minutes or until all the liquid has been absorbed.

Preheat the grill [broiler] to high. Remove the casserole from the oven, remove the lid and sprinkle the cheese over the top. Place the casserole under the grill [broiler] and grill [broil] for 5 minutes or until the cheese has melted and is lightly browned. Remove from the grill [broiler] and serve immediately.

Wild Rice Meat Loaf with Barbecue Sauce

A really unusual meat loaf, Wild Rice Meat Loaf with Barbecue Sauce is ideal for an informal dinner party.

6 SERVINGS

4 oz. [⅔ cup] wild rice, washed, soaked overnight and drained
1 lb. minced [ground] beef
1 lb. minced [ground] veal
4 carrots, scraped and grated
2 onions, finely chopped
1 tablespoon mustard
1½ teaspoons salt

½ teaspoon black pepper
2 eggs, lightly beaten
BARBECUE SAUCE
6 fl. oz. [¾ cup] tomato ketchup
2 tablespoons Worcestershire sauce
2 tablespoons clear honey
1 tablespoon lemon juice
½ teaspoon hot chilli powder
4 fl. oz. [½ cup] water

Preheat the oven to moderate 350°F (Gas Mark 4, 180°C).

In a large mixing bowl, combine all the ingredients for the meat loaf. Mix and knead the ingredients. Spoon the mixture into a 2½-pound loaf tin and smooth the top over with the back of a spoon.

Place the tin in the centre of the oven and bake the loaf for 1¼ to 1½ hours or until the juices run clear when the loaf is pierced with the point of a sharp knife.

Meanwhile, prepare the sauce. In a saucepan, combine all the sauce ingredients. Place the pan over high heat and bring the liquid to the boil, stirring constantly. Boil until the liquid has reduced by one-third. Remove the pan from the heat. Pour the sauce into a warmed sauceboat and keep hot.

Remove the tin from the oven and pour off any fat. Run a knife around the edge of the tin to loosen the sides. Turn the loaf on to a warmed serving dish. Serve immediately, with the sauce.

Yakhni Pulao

LAMB COOKED WITH RICE

This rice pilaff is cooked in a well-flavoured stock called yakhni. Yakhni can be made with any meat or poultry.

4-6 SERVINGS

2 lb. boned leg of lamb, cut into
  1-inch cubes, with bones reserved
  finely pared rind of 1 lemon
½-inch piece fresh root ginger,
  peeled and thinly sliced
2 x 2-inch pieces cinnamon stick
¼ teaspoon grated nutmeg
1 green chilli, chopped
12 black peppercorns
5 fl. oz. [⅝ cup] yogurt
½ teaspoon cayenne pepper
  juice of ½ lemon
1½ teaspoons salt
4 oz. [½ cup] butter
1 onion, finely chopped
4 cloves, bruised
4 whole cardamom pods, bruised
1 teaspoon whole cumin
12 oz. [2 cups] long-grain rice,
  washed, soaked in cold water for
30 minutes and drained

GARNISH

2 tablespoons slivered almonds,
  lightly toasted
1 medium-sized onion, thinly
  sliced and fried until golden
2 tablespoons raisins, lightly fried
2 hard-boiled eggs, quartered

Put the lamb, the reserved lamb bones, the lemon rind, ginger, cinnamon, nutmeg, chilli and peppercorns in a large saucepan. Add enough water to cover the lamb and bones generously and bring to

the boil. When the water comes to the boil, cover the pan, reduce the heat to low and simmer for 40 minutes or until the lamb cubes are tender.

Using a slotted spoon, remove the lamb cubes from the pan and set them aside in a bowl. Re-cover the pan and continue simmering the stock for 2 hours.

Pour the stock through a strainer into a bowl. Discard the contents of the strainer. Set the stock aside to cool. When the stock is cold, skim off and discard the fat on the surface.

Meanwhile, in a small mixing bowl,

combine the yogurt, cayenne, lemon juice and half the salt. Pour this mixture over the lamb cubes and stir well to mix. Cover the bowl and set aside for 2 hours.

In a large saucepan, melt half the butter over moderate heat. When the foam subsides, add the onion and fry, stirring occasionally, for 8 to 10 minutes or until it is golden. Add the cloves, cardamom and cumin and fry, stirring occasionally, for 2 minutes. Add the rice and fry, stirring frequently, for 6 to 8 minutes or until it becomes translucent.

Preheat the oven to very cool 275°F (Gas Mark 1, 140°C).

Meanwhile, pour the stock into a saucepan and bring to the boil. Remove the pan from the heat and pour enough stock over the rice to cover it by a ½-inch. Add the remaining salt and, when the mixture comes to the boil again, cover the pan, reduce the heat to very low and simmer for 15 to 20 minutes or until the rice is tender and all the stock has been absorbed. Remove the pan from the heat.

Meanwhile, in a large frying-pan, melt the remaining butter over moderate heat. When the foam subsides, add the lamb cubes and the yogurt marinade. Fry the lamb, stirring constantly, for 5 minutes. Reduce the heat to low and continue frying, stirring frequently, for 10 minutes. Remove the pan from the heat.

In a baking dish, layer the rice and lamb, beginning and ending with a layer of rice. Cover the dish tightly with foil.

Place the dish in the oven and cook for 20 minutes.

In a small mixing bowl, combine the almonds, onion and raisins. Set aside.

Remove the dish from the oven. Sprinkle over the garnish and arrange the eggs over the top. Serve immediately.

Yunnan Quick-Fried Prawns or Shrimps on Crackling Rice

☆ ☆   ① ①

Serve this adaptation of a Chinese dish as part of a traditional Chinese meal or as a delightfully exotic supper or lunch dish.

4 SERVINGS
8 oz. prawns or shrimps, weighed after shelling
8 oz. boned chicken breast, cut into 2-inch cubes
2 teaspoons salt
1 teaspoon white pepper
1 tablespoon cornflour [cornstarch]
1 lb. [6 cups] cooked rice

Yunnan Quick-Fried Prawns or Shrimps on Crackling Rice is an exotic dish from China.

sufficient vegetable oil for deep-frying
SAUCE
2 tablespoons vegetable oil
1 onion, chopped
5 fl. oz. [⅝ cup] beef stock
2 tablespoons tomato purée
1½ tablespoons soy sauce
1½ tablespoons sugar
1½ tablespoons wine vinegar
2 tablespoons dry sherry
1 teaspoon chilli sauce
4 teaspoons cornflour [cornstarch]

Preheat the oven to very cool 275°F (Gas Mark 1, 140°C).

Sprinkle the prawns or shrimps and chicken cubes with the salt, pepper and cornflour [cornstarch] and, using your fingers, rub them into the shellfish and chicken. Set aside.

Place the rice in an ovenproof dish and put the dish in the oven. Dry out the rice for 15 to 20 minutes or until it is crisp.

Meanwhile, make the sauce. In a large frying-pan, heat the oil over moderate heat. When the oil is hot, add the onion and fry, stirring occasionally, for 3 minutes. Add all the remaining sauce ingredients and mix well to blend. Cook the sauce, stirring constantly, for 2 minutes or until it becomes thick and translucent. Remove the pan from the heat and set aside.

Fill a large, deep-frying pan one-third full with vegetable oil. Set the pan over moderate heat and heat the oil until it reaches 360°F on a deep-fat thermometer or until a small cube of stale bread dropped into the oil turns golden brown in 50 seconds.

Place the prawns or shrimps and chicken cubes in a deep-frying basket and lower them into the oil. Deep-fry them for 1 minute then remove the pan from the heat. Remove the basket from the pan and set it over kitchen paper towels to drain. Transfer the prawns or shrimps and chicken cubes to the sauce in the frying-pan and return the frying-pan to moderate heat. Cook the mixture, stirring constantly, for 2 minutes.

Meanwhile, return the deep-frying pan to moderate heat and reheat the oil until it reaches 350°F on a deep-fat thermometer or until a small cube of stale bread dropped into the oil turns golden brown in 55 seconds.

Remove the rice from the oven, place it in a narrow-meshed deep-frying basket and lower it into the oil. Fry the rice for 1½ minutes, then remove it from the oil and drain on kitchen paper towels.

Arrange the rice on a warmed serving dish and pour over the prawns or shrimps, chicken cubes and sauce. Serve at once.

Pasta

Pasta, a name that is almost synonymous with Italian cuisine, is a farinaceous product made from flour, water and sometimes eggs. The flour used is made from a hard or durum wheat with a high gluten content, which gives the dough its slightly brittle consistency.

Pasta is usually made commercially these days, although some types — most particularly egg noodles, ravioli and gnocchi — are still traditionally made at home. In the factories, machines are used to produce the different shapes and sizes of pasta sold to the public as the familiar cannelloni, farfalle, fettuccine, fusilli, lasagne, macaroni, manicotti, noodles, ravioli, spaghetti, tagliatelli, tortellini, vermicelli, zite. Spinach is sometimes added to the basic pasta dough — thus fettuccine verdi and lasagne verdi.

Pasta is always served with a sauce of some kind — even though it may be as simple as melted butter and grated cheese. In Italy pasta is served as the course before the main, usually meat, course of the meal, although in other parts of Europe and in the United States pasta is more often served as a main course. The lighter, smaller pasta, such as vermicelli, is often used in soups, and the heavier pasta, such as macaroni, can also be made into substantial sweet or savoury puddings.

A selection of some of the more popular types of pasta, including spinach pasta.

Cannelloni Filled with a Savoury Meat and Spinach Mixture with Tomato and Cream Sauces

  ⋈ ⋈

This famous Italian dish is economical and very tasty. Serve with a tossed mixed salad for a delicious supper.

4 SERVINGS

TOMATO SAUCE
2 tablespoons olive oil
1 small onion, finely chopped
14 oz. canned peeled Italian tomatoes
2½ oz. canned tomato purée
½ tablespoon finely chopped fresh basil or ½ teaspoon dried basil
1 teaspoon chopped fresh oregano or ½ teaspoon dried oregano
1 teaspoon sugar
½ teaspoon salt
½ teaspoon freshly ground black pepper

FILLING
1½ tablespoons olive oil
1 tablespoon butter
1 small onion, finely chopped
2 garlic cloves, finely chopped
8 oz. lean minced [ground] beef
6 oz. fresh spinach, cooked, drained, squeezed and finely chopped or a small packet frozen chopped spinach (thawed)
1 oz. [¼ cup] Parmesan cheese, grated
1½ tablespoons double [heavy] cream
1 egg
1 teaspoon chopped fresh oregano or ½ teaspoon dried oregano
¼ teaspoon salt
½ teaspoon black pepper

CREAM SAUCE
1 oz. [2 tablespoons] butter
4 tablespoons flour
5 fl. oz. [⅝ cup] plus 2 tablespoons milk, warmed
3 tablespoons double [heavy] cream
¼ teaspoon salt
⅛ teaspoon white pepper

PASTA
1 teaspoon salt
8 oz. cannelloni, cut into rectangles 3 inches by 4 inches
3 oz. [¾ cup] Parmesan cheese, grated
1 tablespoon butter, cut into small pieces

Cannelloni Filled with a Savoury Meat and Spinach Mixture with Tomato and Cream Sauces is a filling main dish from Italy.

To make the tomato sauce, in a medium-sized saucepan heat the oil over moderate heat. Add the onion and fry it for 5 to 7 minutes, or until it is soft and translucent but not brown. Stir in the tomatoes with the can juice, tomato purée, basil, oregano, sugar, salt and pepper. Reduce the heat to low, cover and simmer the sauce for 40 minutes, stirring occasionally.

Remove the pan from the heat and set aside.

To make the filling, in a large frying-pan heat the oil with the butter over moderate heat. Add the onion and garlic and fry, stirring occasionally, for 5 to 7 minutes, or until the onion is soft. Add the meat. Cook for 10 minutes or until the meat is browned, stirring occasionally. Add the spinach and, stirring, cook for 3 to 4 minutes or until all the moisture has evaporated.

Transfer the meat and spinach mixture to a medium-sized bowl. Add the Parmesan, cream, egg, oregano, salt and pepper. Mix well with a spoon and set aside.

Now prepare the cream sauce. In a small saucepan, melt the butter over moderate heat. Remove the pan from the heat and, with a wooden spoon, stir in the flour. Gradually stir in 5 fluid ounces [⅝ cup] of the milk and the cream. Return the pan to the heat. Cook,

Elegant Egg Noodles with Pork Sauce is an unusual dish from China and the sauce has a delightfully sweet-sour flavour.

stirring constantly, until the sauce comes to the boil. The sauce will be very thick. Remove the pan from the heat and add the salt and pepper. Pour the 2 tablespoons of milk over the top of the sauce to prevent a skin forming and set the pan aside.

Preheat the oven to fairly hot 375°F (Gas Mark 5, 190°C).

In a large saucepan, bring 3 to 4 pints [2½ quarts] of water to the boil over high heat. Add the teaspoon of salt with the cannelloni pieces and cook them for 8 to 10 minutes or until the cannelloni is 'al dente' or just tender. With a slotted spoon, remove the pasta from the pan and place it on a dampened cloth to drain.

When the cannelloni is cool enough to handle, place a tablespoonful of the filling in the centre of each pasta rectangle and roll them up.

Pour a thin layer of tomato sauce into the bottom of a large shallow ovenproof dish. Place the cannelloni in the dish in a single or double layer.

Stir the milk into the cream sauce and spoon over the cannelloni. Pour the remaining tomato sauce over the top of the mixture. Sprinkle with the grated Parmesan cheese and dot with the tablespoon of butter.

Place the dish in the oven and bake the cannelloni for 30 minutes, or until the

sauce is bubbling and the cheese has melted.

Serve immediately.

Egg Noodles with Pork Sauce

A variation on a traditional Chinese recipe, this dish has an interesting meat sauce with a rather unusual sweet-sour flavour. The garnish has a strong garlic flavour. Thin carrot sticks would make a good accompaniment.

4 SERVINGS

1 large cucumber
3 spring onions [scallions], finely chopped
4 garlic cloves, finely chopped
3 tablespoons vegetable oil
1 lb. minced [ground] pork
2 tablespoons dry sherry
2 tablespoons Worcestershire sauce
1 tablespoon soy sauce
1 large onion, finely chopped
2 teaspoons soft brown sugar
3 fl. oz. [⅜ cup] chicken stock
12 oz. egg noodles

Peel the cucumber and cut it in half lengthways. With the tip of a teaspoon, scoop out the seeds. With a sharp kitchen knife, cut the cucumber lengthways into ¼-inch slices. Cut each of these slices into strips 2 inches long.

Arrange the cucumber and onions [scallions] on a serving plate and sprinkle with the garlic. Set the garnishes aside while you make the sauce.

Warm a large frying-pan over high heat. Add 2 tablespoons of oil and heat for about 1 minute or until the oil is very hot. If the oil begins to smoke, reduce the heat to moderate.

Add the pork and fry it, stirring constantly, for about 5 minutes or until the pork begins to brown.

Stir in the sherry, Worcestershire sauce, soy sauce, onion, sugar and chicken stock.

Bring the liquid to the boil and cook for 10 to 15 minutes, or until all the liquid has evaporated. Cover the pan tightly and remove it from the heat. Set the pan in a warm place to keep the pork sauce warm.

Fill a large saucepan two-thirds full of water and bring it to the boil over high heat. Add the noodles and boil for 6 to 8 minutes or until they are just tender but not mushy. Stir occasionally to prevent the noodles from sticking to each other. Drain the noodles and toss in the remaining tablespoon of oil.

Place the noodles in a large, warmed serving dish and cover with the pork sauce. Sprinkle over some of the spring onions [scallions] and serve with the remaining garnishes.

Fettuccine Alfredo

This delicious mixture of pasta with cheese and cream is especially popular in the United States. Fettuccine Alfredo may be served on its own or accompanied by a mixed green salad.

4 SERVINGS

2 pints [5 cups] water
2 teaspoons salt
1 lb. fettuccine
2 oz. [¼ cup] butter
4 oz. [1 cup] Parmesan cheese, grated
8 fl. oz. double cream [1 cup heavy cream]
½ teaspoon freshly ground white pepper

In a large saucepan, bring the water and salt to the boil over high heat.

Drop the fettuccine into the water. Reduce the heat to moderate and cook the fettuccine for 5 to 7 minutes, or until it is 'al dente' or just tender.

Remove the pan from the heat and drain the fettuccine in a colander.

Transfer the fettuccine to a warmed serving dish.

Add the butter, cheese, cream and pepper to the fettuccine and, using two forks, toss the mixture well.

Serve at once.

Fettuccine alla Romana

A tasty, colourful Italian dish, Fettuccine alla Romana is perfect for a family meal or an informal dinner party.

4 SERVINGS

2 oz. [¼ cup] plus 1 tablespoon
  butter
1 medium-sized onion, chopped
1 garlic clove, chopped
14 oz. canned peeled Italian tomatoes
4 oz. mushrooms, wiped clean and
  sliced
1½ teaspoons salt
¼ teaspoon freshly ground black
  pepper
2 fl. oz. [¼ cup] dry red wine
1 teaspoon sugar
2 pints [5 cups] water
1 lb. fettuccine
2 tablespoons grated Parmesan
  cheese

In a large, deep frying-pan, melt 2 ounces [¼ cup] of the butter over moderate heat. When the foam subsides, add the onion and garlic to the pan and fry them, stirring occasionally, for 5 to 7 minutes, or until the onion is soft and translucent but not brown.

Add the tomatoes with the can juice, mushrooms, ½ teaspoon of salt, the pepper, wine and sugar. Stir well and bring the liquid to the boil. Cover the pan, reduce the heat to low and simmer gently for 20 minutes.

Meanwhile, prepare the fettuccine. In a large saucepan bring the water to the boil over high heat. Add the remaining salt and the fettuccine. Reduce the heat

to moderate, boil for 5 to 7 minutes, or until the fettuccine is 'al dente' or just tender.

Remove the pan from the heat and drain the fettuccine in a colander. Transfer it to a warmed serving dish and stir in the remaining butter. Pour over the sauce and sprinkle with the Parmesan cheese.

Serve immediately.

Gnocchi al Forno Napoletana
ITALIAN BAKED DUMPLINGS WITH
TOMATO SAUCE

This tasty dish is popular in the region of Southern Italy around Naples. With its delicious tomato sauce, serve it for a family supper or lunch, accompanied by a tossed mixed salad and lots of crusty bread and butter.

4 SERVINGS

GNOCCHI
4 egg yolks
2 teaspoons sugar
2 oz. [½ cup] flour
2 tablespoons cornflour [cornstarch]
¼ teaspoon salt
2 oz. [¼ cup] plus 1 teaspoon butter,
  melted
4 oz. [1 cup] Parmesan cheese,
  finely grated
15 fl. oz. [1⅞ cups] milk
SAUCE
1 oz. [2 tablespoons] butter
2 tablespoons olive oil
1 medium-sized onion, finely
  chopped
2 garlic cloves, crushed
2 lb. canned peeled Italian tomatoes

Fettuccine alla Romana is a mixture of noodles, tomatoes, mushrooms, red wine and cheese.

2 teaspoons tomato purée
1 bay leaf
1 tablespoon dry vermouth
  (optional)
½ teaspoon salt
¼ teaspoon freshly ground black
  pepper
1 teaspoon sugar
1 tablespoon finely chopped fresh
  parsley

First, make the gnocchi. Place the egg yolks and sugar in a medium-sized saucepan and, using a wire whisk or a rotary beater, beat the mixture until it is creamy and pale.

Carefully sift the flour, cornflour [cornstarch], and salt into a small mixing bowl. Gradually add the flour mixture to the egg yolk mixture, beating constantly with a wooden spoon until the mixture is thick and smooth. Stir in 2 ounces [¼ cup] of the melted butter, then add 3 ounces [¾ cup] of the grated cheese.

Place the saucepan over moderately low heat. Gradually add the milk, stirring constantly with the wooden spoon. Cook the mixture for 3 to 4 minutes or until it is thick and smooth. Remove the pan from the heat.

Rinse a large baking sheet with water. Turn the gnocchi mixture on to the sheet and smooth out the top with a flat-bladed knife. The mixture should be about half an inch thick. Place the baking sheet in the refrigerator and chill the mixture for 30 minutes.

Meanwhile, make the tomato sauce. In a medium-sized saucepan, melt the butter with the olive oil over moderate heat. When the foam subsides, add the onion and garlic to the pan and fry, stirring occasionally, for 5 to 7 minutes or until the onion is soft and translucent but not brown. Add all of the remaining sauce ingredients and bring the mixture to the boil, stirring constantly with a wooden spoon. Reduce the heat to moderately low, cover the pan and simmer the sauce for 30 minutes or until it is rich and thick.

Preheat the oven to fairly hot 375°F (Gas Mark 5, 190°C).

With the remaining teaspoon of butter, lightly grease a medium-sized baking dish. Set the dish aside.

Remove the baking sheet from the refrigerator and cut the gnocchi into squares. Place them, overlapping slightly, in the prepared baking dish. Sprinkle the remaining cheese on top. Put the dish into the oven and bake for 15 to 20 minutes or until the top is golden brown and the cheese has melted.

Remove the baking dish from the oven and serve the gnocchi immediately, either with the sauce poured over the top, or served separately in a warmed sauceboat or jug.

Gnocchi Verdi
SPINACH DUMPLINGS

These tasty Italian dumplings make an unusual first course to an Italian meal. Gnocchi Verdi may also be served as a tasty lunch or supper for the family accompanied by grilled [broiled] bacon and, if liked, a mushroom sauce.

4-6 SERVINGS

1½ lb. spinach, trimmed and washed
3 teaspoons salt
2 oz. [¼ cup] butter
1 medium-sized onion, very finely chopped
8 oz. [1 cup] ricotta cheese
½ teaspoon white pepper
¼ teaspoon grated nutmeg
2 eggs
4 tablespoons grated Parmesan cheese
4 oz. [1 cup] flour
2 oz. [¼ cup] butter, melted

Put the spinach into a large saucepan.

Pour over enough water just to cover the spinach. Add 1 teaspoon of salt and place the pan over moderate heat. Cook the spinach for 7 to 12 minutes, or until it is tender. Remove the pan from the heat and drain the spinach in a colander, pressing down well on the spinach with a wooden spoon to extract all of the excess liquid.

Transfer the spinach to a chopping board. With a sharp knife, finely chop the spinach.

In a large saucepan, melt the butter over moderate heat. When the foam subsides, add the onion to the pan and cook, stirring occasionally, for 5 to 7 minutes, or until it is soft and translucent but not brown. Add the chopped spinach to the pan and, with a wooden spoon, stir in the ricotta cheese, 1 teaspoon of the remaining salt, the pepper and the nutmeg. Beat until the mixture is smooth. Reduce the heat to low and cook for 5 minutes, stirring frequently.

Remove the pan from the heat and beat in the eggs, half the grated Parmesan cheese and the flour. Turn the mixture into a mixing bowl and leave it to cool. Then place the bowl in the refrigerator

Gnocchi dumplings are still widely made at home in Italy—and much enjoyed! You can see why, when you taste delicious Gnocchi al Forno Napoletana.

to chill for 2 to 3 hours or until the mixture is firm and 'set'.

Remove the mixture from the refrigerator and turn it out on to a lightly floured board. Divide the mixture into large walnut-sized pieces and, using the palms of your hands, carefully roll them into balls.

Pour 1 tablespoon of the melted butter into a shallow flameproof dish and sprinkle with 1 tablespoon of the remaining grated Parmesan cheese. Set the dish aside.

Half fill a large saucepan with cold water and add the remaining salt. Place the pan over high heat and bring the water to the boil. Reduce the heat to moderate and, when the water comes to the boil again, drop in the balls, a few at a time. Simmer until they rise to the surface. With a slotted spoon, remove the gnocchi from the pan and drain them on kitchen paper towels. Place them in the flameproof dish and keep them hot while you cook the remaining balls in the same way.

Preheat the grill [broiler] to moderately high.

Pour the remaining melted butter and sprinkle the remaining Parmesan cheese over the gnocchi. Place the dish under the grill [broiler] and grill [broil] the gnocchi for 5 minutes, or until the cheese is golden brown.

Serve immediately, straight from the flameproof dish.

Fusilli Noodles with Tomatoes and Cheese

This simple and absolutely delicious Italian dish is ideal for a quick and filling family meal. Fusilli are a curly, spiral type of spaghetti which go particularly well with this sauce. If they are not available, however, spaghetti may be substituted.

4 SERVINGS

2 tablespoons vegetable oil
1 medium-sized onion, finely
   chopped
14 oz. canned peeled tomatoes
2 tablespoons tomato purée
1 teaspoon dried oregano
1½ teaspoons salt
½ teaspoon black pepper
1 lb. fusilli noodles
4 oz. Bel Paese cheese, cut into
   small pieces
2 oz. [½ cup] Parmesan cheese,
   grated

In a medium-sized frying-pan, heat the oil over moderate heat. When the oil is hot, add the onion and fry it, stirring occasionally, for 5 to 7 minutes, or until it is soft and translucent but not brown.

Add the tomatoes with the can juice, the tomato purée, oregano, ½ teaspoon of the salt and the pepper. Stir well and

bring the liquid to the boil over high heat. Reduce the heat to low, cover the pan and simmer for 20 minutes, stirring occasionally.

Meanwhile, half-fill a large saucepan with water. Add the remaining salt and bring the water to the boil over high heat. Reduce the heat to moderate and drop the noodles into the water. Cook for 8 to 10 minutes, depending on whether you like your pasta 'al dente' or just tender.

Remove the pan from the heat. Drain the noodles in a colander and return them to the saucepan.

Add the tomato sauce and cheeses to the pan. Place the pan over low heat and toss the noodles with two forks until the cheeses have melted.

Turn the noodles and sauce into a warmed serving dish and serve the mixture at once.

Macaroni Cheese

Despite its Italian origin, macaroni forms the basis of one of the most typical of English supper dishes, Macaroni Cheese. A simple-to-make economical dish, Macaroni Cheese served with a tossed green salad and crusty bread makes an absolutely delicious meal.

The unusual sauce is what makes Macaroni and Green Pea Sauce really special. Use fresh peas if possible.

2-3 SERVINGS

1 oz. [2 tablespoons] plus 1 teaspoon
   butter
1 pint [2½ cups] water
1½ teaspoons salt
8 oz. macaroni
15 fl. oz. [1⅞ cups] béchamel sauce
½ teaspoon prepared mustard
¼ teaspoon white pepper
⅛ teaspoon cayenne pepper
4 oz. [1 cup] Cheddar cheese,
   grated
1 oz. [⅓ cup] fine dry breadcrumbs

Preheat the oven to fairly hot 400°F (Gas Mark 6, 200°C). With the teaspoon of butter, lightly grease a medium-sized ovenproof baking dish and set aside.

Pour the water into a medium-sized saucepan and add 1 teaspoon of the salt. Place the pan over high heat and bring the water to the boil. Reduce the heat to moderate and add the macaroni. Cook the macaroni for 8 to 10 minutes, or until it is 'al dente' or just tender. Remove the pan from the heat and drain the macaroni in a colander. Set aside.

In a large mixing bowl, combine the

40

Macaroni Shells with Mussels makes a delightful informal meal, served with crusty bread and white wine.

remaining salt, béchamel sauce, mustard, the pepper, cayenne and 2 ounces [½ cup] of the cheese, mixing well. Add the macaroni to the mixture and stir well to blend.

Pour the mixture into the prepared dish. In a small bowl, combine the remaining cheese and breadcrumbs and sprinkle the mixture over the macaroni mixture in the dish. Cut the remaining butter into small pieces and dot over the top of the cheese and breadcrumb mixture.

Place the dish in the oven and bake for 15 to 20 minutes, or until the top is crisp and golden brown.

Remove the dish from the oven and serve at once.

Macaroni with Green Pea Sauce

This sauce is only really good when made with fresh green peas and may be served with most boiled pasta. Macaroni with Green Pea Sauce may be served as a supper dish or, in smaller quantities, as a first course to an Italian meal.

4 SERVINGS

2 tablespoons olive oil
1 medium-sized onion, chopped
4 slices lean bacon, chopped
½ teaspoon dried basil
⅛ teaspoon dried dill
1 teaspoon salt
½ teaspoon black pepper
1½ lb. fresh green peas, weighed after shelling
8 fl. oz. [1 cup] water
4 fl. oz. single cream [½ cup light cream]
12 oz. macaroni, cooked for 8 to 10 minutes, drained and kept warm in a colander over a pan of hot water
1 oz. [2 tablespoons] butter
2 oz. [½ cup] Parmesan cheese, grated

In a medium-sized saucepan, heat the oil over moderate heat. When the oil is hot, add the onion and the bacon and fry, stirring occasionally, for 5 to 7 minutes or until the onion is soft and translucent but not brown and the bacon is crisp.

Add the basil, dill, salt, pepper and peas. Pour in the water and bring to the boil. Reduce the heat to low and simmer the mixture for 10 to 12 minutes or until

the peas are tender.

Remove the pan from the heat. Purée the contents of the pan through a food mill or in an electric blender.

Return the puréed sauce to the pan and stir in the cream. Place the pan over low heat and, stirring occasionally, simmer the sauce for 2 minutes or until it is hot. Taste the sauce and add more salt and pepper if necessary. Pour the sauce into a warmed sauceboat. Keep warm.

In a saucepan, combine the macaroni and butter. Place the pan over low heat and toss the pasta in the butter.

Place the buttered macaroni in a warmed serving dish.

Serve immediately with the sauce and cheese handed round separately.

Macaroni Shells with Mussels

Serve this delicious and filling Italian dish with crusty bread and a tossed mixed salad for a family lunch or supper. Chianti would be an excellent accompaniment.

4 SERVINGS

2 fl. oz. [¼ cup] olive oil
2 garlic cloves, finely chopped
1 lb. tomatoes, blanched, peeled

and chopped
8 oz. mushrooms, wiped clean and sliced
1 teaspoon dried basil
½ teaspoon dried oregano
½ teaspoon salt
½ teaspoon black pepper
2 tablespoons tomato purée
1 quart mussels, scrubbed, steamed, removed from their shells and the cooking liquid reserved
8 oz. macaroni shells, cooked for 8 to 10 minutes, drained and kept hot

In a large frying-pan, heat the oil over moderate heat. When the oil is hot, add the garlic and fry, stirring constantly, for 2 minutes. Add the tomatoes, mushrooms, basil, oregano, salt, pepper and tomato purée and fry, stirring occasionally, for 5 minutes or until the mixture begins to boil. Add the mussels, with the reserved cooking liquid, and cook, stirring occasionally, for 2 to 3 minutes or until the mussels are heated through. Remove the pan from the heat.

Place the macaroni in a warmed serving dish. Pour over the mussel sauce and serve at once.

Chow Mein

Chow Mein is surely one of the best known of Chinese dishes — and one which is often badly made in the West. This recipe is easy to prepare and truly delicious.

4 SERVINGS

1 teaspoon salt
1 lb. egg noodles or spaghetti
8 oz. French beans, trimmed and halved
4 tablespoons vegetable oil
1 medium-sized onion, very thinly sliced
1 garlic clove, crushed
4 oz. chicken meat (breast or leg), finely shredded
2 tablespoons soy sauce
1 teaspoon sugar
1 tablespoon sherry
1½ tablespoons butter
3 tablespoons chicken stock
½ chicken stock cube, crumbled

Half-fill a large saucepan with water and bring it to the boil over high heat. Add the salt and noodles or spaghetti. When the water returns to the boil, reduce the heat to moderate and cook the noodles for 5 to 8 minutes, or the spaghetti for 10 to 12 minutes, or until they are 'al dente' or just tender. Remove the pan from the heat and drain the noodles or spaghetti in a colander. Set aside and keep warm.

Half-fill a medium-sized saucepan with water and bring it to the boil over high heat. Add the beans and boil them for 5 minutes. Remove the pan from the heat and drain the beans in a colander. Set aside.

In a large frying-pan, heat the oil over moderate heat. Add the onion and garlic and fry, stirring constantly, for 2 minutes. Add the chicken and stir-fry for 1 minute. Add the beans, soy sauce, sugar and sherry and continue to stir-fry for 1½ minutes.

With a slotted spoon, remove the bean and chicken mixture from the pan and set it aside in a bowl. Keep warm.

Add the butter, chicken stock and stock cube to the oil remaining in the frying-pan. When the butter has melted, add the noodles or spaghetti. Cook, stirring and turning constantly, for 2 minutes or until the pasta is heated through.

Add half of the bean and chicken mixture and mix well. Transfer the mixture

This simple dish of noodles cooked with ham, garlic sausage and tomatoes, makes a tasty supper. Serve Noodles with Ham with salad.

to a warmed serving dish. Set aside and keep warm.

Return the remaining bean and chicken mixture to the frying-pan and increase the heat to high. Fry, stirring constantly, for 1 minute, adding more oil or soy sauce to the pan if necessary.

Remove the pan from the heat and spoon the bean and chicken mixture over the pasta mixture.

Serve immediately.

Noodles with Breadcrumbs and Cheese

An easy-to-prepare supper dish for the family, Noodles with Breadcrumbs and Cheese could be served with French beans and a tomato salad.

6 SERVINGS

1 lb. noodles, cooked for 5 to 8 minutes, drained and kept hot
2 oz. [¼ cup] butter, cut into small pieces
1 oz. [¼ cup] Parmesan cheese, finely grated
2 oz. [½ cup] Gruyère cheese, finely grated
3 tablespoons dry white breadcrumbs
¼ teaspoon freshly ground black pepper

Preheat the grill [broiler] to high.

Place the noodles in a heatproof serving dish. Stir in half the butter. Sprinkle the grated cheeses, breadcrumbs and pepper over the noodles. Dot the top of the dish with the remaining butter.

Place the dish under the grill [broiler] and grill [broil] for 3 to 4 minutes or until the cheeses have melted and the top is a light golden brown.

Remove the dish from under the heat and serve immediately.

Noodles with Ham

A quick supper dish, Noodles with Ham may be sprinkled with grated Parmesan cheese just before serving.

4-6 SERVINGS

1 lb. noodles, cooked for 5 to 8 minutes, drained and kept warm
2 oz. [¼ cup] butter, cut into small pieces
½ teaspoon salt
½ teaspoon freshly ground black pepper
1 teaspoon dried basil
2 oz. prosciutto, cut into thin strips

6 oz. cooked lean ham, cut into thin strips
1 small garlic sausage, cut into thin strips
2 large tomatoes, blanched, peeled, seeded and cut into strips

In a large saucepan, heat the noodles and butter over very low heat. When the butter has melted, using two forks, toss the noodles until they are coated with the butter. Add the salt, pepper, basil, prosciutto, ham, sausage and tomatoes. Increase the heat to moderate and cook the noodle mixture, stirring frequently with a wooden spoon, for 6 to 8 minutes or until it is very hot.

Remove the pan from the heat. Transfer the noodle mixture to a heated large serving dish and serve it immediately.

Noodles with Onions

Noodles with Onions complements the rich taste of a beef pot roast, or goulasch very well.

4 SERVINGS

1 lb. noodles, cooked for 5 to 8 minutes and drained
3 oz. [⅜ cup] butter
½ teaspoon freshly ground black pepper
¼ teaspoon grated nutmeg
2 small onions, thinly sliced and pushed out into rings

Preheat the oven to warm 300°F (Gas Mark 2, 150°C).

Place the noodles in a large shallow ovenproof dish.

Cut 1 ounce [2 tablespoons] of the butter into small pieces and dot the noodles with them. Sprinkle the pepper and nutmeg over the noodles and place the dish in the oven. Bake the mixture for 10 minutes.

Meanwhile, in a small frying-pan, melt the remaining butter over moderate heat. When the foam subsides, add the onions and cook them, stirring occasionally, for 5 to 7 minutes or until they are soft and translucent but not brown. Remove the pan from the heat.

Remove the dish of noodles from the oven and stir well. Pour the onion mixture over the noodles. Increase the oven temperature to moderate 350°F (Gas Mark 4, 180°C). Return the dish to the oven and bake the noodles for a further 15 to 20 minutes or until the onions are crisp.

Remove from the oven and serve immediately.

Peking Noodles with Meat Sauce and Shredded Vegetables

This Chinese peasant dish is gradually becoming a classic. Each diner is given a bowl of noodles to which he adds as much meat sauce and shredded vegetables as he likes.

4 SERVINGS

1 teaspoon salt
1 lb. noodles or spaghetti
3 tablespoons vegetable oil
1 onion, thinly sliced
2 garlic cloves, crushed
2 slices fresh root ginger, peeled and finely chopped, or ½ teaspoon ground ginger
12 oz. lean pork or beef, minced [ground]
1 tablespoon sesame oil
5 tablespoons soy sauce
2 tablespoons dry sherry
1 tablespoon sugar
1 tablespoon cornflour [cornstarch] dissolved in 4 tablespoons chicken stock

SHREDDED VEGETABLES

3 to 4 oz. (or a heaped side-dishful) shredded cabbage, blanched for 4 minutes and drained
3 to 4 oz. (or a heaped side-dishful) shredded carrots, blanched for 4 minutes and drained
3 to 4 oz. (or a heaped side-dishful) bean sprouts, blanched for 1 minute and drained
3 to 4 oz. (or a heaped side-dishful) shredded cucumber
2 to 3 oz. (or a saucerful) shredded radishes
1 to 2 oz. (or a saucerful) mixed pickles
1 to 2 oz. (or a saucerful) chutney

Arrange the shredded vegetables, pickles and chutney on individual serving dishes. Set aside.

Half-fill a large saucepan with water and bring it to the boil over high heat. Add the salt and the noodles or spaghetti. When the water returns to the boil, reduce the heat to moderate and cook the noodles for 5 to 8 minutes, or the spaghetti for 10 to 12 minutes, or until they are 'al dente' or just tender. Remove the pan from the heat and drain the pasta in a colander. Set aside and keep warm.

In a large frying-pan, heat the vegetable oil over moderate heat. Add the onion, garlic and ginger and fry, stirring constantly, for 1½ minutes. Add the pork or beef and stir-fry for 5 minutes, or until the meat loses its pinkness.

Stir in the sesame oil, soy sauce, sherry and sugar and continue to stir-fry for 3 minutes. Add the dissolved cornflour [cornstarch] and continue to cook, stirring constantly, until the meat sauce thickens and becomes glossy.

Remove the pan from the heat and transfer the meat sauce to a warmed serving bowl. Keep warm.

Divide the noodles or spaghetti between four serving bowls. Serve immediately, with the meat sauce and vegetables.

Wienerwurst and Noodle Casserole

An unusual dish, Wienerwurst and Noodle Casserole makes a sustaining family supper or lunch. Serve with mixed salad. If wienerwurst sausages are not available, frankfurters may be used instead.

3-4 SERVINGS

3 oz. [⅜ cup] butter
1 onion, finely chopped
1 garlic clove, crushed
4 courgettes [zucchini], trimmed and cut into ½-inch lengths
1 teaspoon salt
2 teaspoons black pepper
1 lb. wienerwurst sausages, cooked in hot water for 10 minutes, drained and cut into 1-inch lengths
1 oz. [¼ cup] flour
10 fl. oz. [1¼ cups] milk
4 oz. [1 cup] Gruyère cheese, grated
¼ teaspoon red pepper flakes
8 oz. egg noodles, cooked for 5 to 8 minutes and drained

In a large frying-pan, melt 2 ounces [¼ cup] of the butter over moderate heat. When the foam subsides, add the onion, garlic and courgettes [zucchini] and fry, stirring and turning occasionally, for 5 to 7 minutes or until the onion is soft and translucent but not brown. Add the salt, 1 teaspoon of pepper and the wienerwurst and continue to cook, turning occasionally, for 5 minutes or until the courgettes [zucchini] are cooked and tender. Remove the pan from the heat.

Preheat the oven to moderate 350°F (Gas Mark 4, 180°C).

In a medium-sized saucepan, melt the remaining butter over moderate heat. Remove the pan from the heat and, using a wooden spoon, stir in the flour to make a smooth paste. Gradually add the milk, stirring constantly to avoid lumps. Return the pan to low heat and cook, stirring constantly, for 2 minutes. Stir in 3 ounces [¾ cup] of the grated cheese, the

remaining pepper and the red pepper flakes and cook, stirring constantly, for a further 1 minute or until the cheese has melted and the sauce is smooth and thick. Stir in the cooked noodles.

Spoon the noodles and the wienerwurst mixture into a large baking dish and, using two large spoons, stir and toss to mix well. Sprinkle over the remaining grated cheese. Place the dish in the oven and bake the mixture for 15 to 20 minutes or until the top is brown and bubbling.

Remove from the oven and serve.

Yangchow Noodles

Yangchow Noodles consist of thinly sliced pork, spring onions [scallions] and celery in a slightly sweet-sour sauce served on a bed of succulent noodles.

3 SERVINGS

3 tablespoons vegetable oil
1 lb. lean pork, thinly sliced
3 tablespoons chopped spring

SAUCE

1 tablespoon olive oil
1 onion, finely chopped
28 oz. canned peeled tomatoes, drained and chopped
½ teaspoon dried basil
½ teaspoon dried oregano
½ teaspoon dried thyme
½ teaspoon salt
½ teaspoon white pepper
1 teaspoon sugar

STUFFING

12 oz. ham, minced [ground]
1 teaspoon chopped fresh parsley
2 garlic cloves, crushed
2 tablespoons olive oil
1 egg, lightly beaten

PASTA

1 teaspoon salt
1¼ lb. rigatoni
1 tablespoon olive oil
4 oz. [1 cup] Parmesan cheese, grated

First make the sauce. In a medium-sized saucepan, heat the olive oil over moderate heat. Add the onion and, stirring frequently, fry for about 5 to 7 minutes or until it is soft and translucent but not brown. Add the tomatoes, basil, oregano, thyme, salt, pepper and sugar. Stir to mix, cover the pan and simmer for 30 minutes or until the sauce is thick. Taste and add more seasoning if necessary.

Meanwhile, make the stuffing. In a medium-sized mixing bowl, combine the ham with the parsley and garlic. In a medium-sized frying-pan, heat the olive oil over moderate heat. Add the ham mixture and fry for 10 minutes, turning constantly with a wooden spoon so that it browns evenly. Put the mixture in a bowl and leave it to cool. When it is cold mix in the egg.

Preheat the oven to warm 325°F (Gas Mark 3, 170°C).

Half-fill a large saucepan with water, add 1 teaspoon of salt and bring to the boil over high heat. Drop in the rigatoni and cook for 10 to 12 minutes or until it is 'al dente' or just tender. Drain and leave to cool for a few minutes. Using a small teaspoon, carefully stuff the rigatoni with the meat mixture.

Grease an ovenproof dish with the tablespoon of olive oil and put the stuffed pasta in it. Cover the dish with aluminium foil and put it in the oven to bake for 30 minutes or until the mixture is cooked.

Reheat the sauce and pour it over the pasta. Sprinkle with the Parmesan cheese and serve immediately.

---

onions [scallions]
2 celery stalks, thinly sliced
4 fl. oz. [½ cup] chicken stock
1 tablespoon soy sauce
½ teaspoon cayenne pepper
4 oz. button mushrooms, wiped clean and thinly sliced
1 tablespoon soft brown sugar
2 teaspoons cornflour [cornstarch], dissolved in 1 tablespoon water
8 oz. egg noodles

In a large frying-pan, heat 2 tablespoons of the oil over high heat.

Add the pork and fry, stirring constantly, for about 8 minutes or until it is evenly browned. Reduce the heat to moderate and add the spring onions [scallions] and celery. Fry, stirring occasionally, for a further 5 minutes. Stir in the stock, soy sauce, cayenne, mushrooms, sugar and the cornflour [cornstarch] mixture.

Bring the liquid to the boil, stirring constantly, and cook for 10 minutes or until the sauce has thickened. Cover the pan tightly and remove it from the heat. Keep hot while you cook the noodles.

Fill a large saucepan two-thirds full with water and bring it to the boil over high heat. Add the noodles and boil for 5 to 8 minutes or until they are 'al dente' or just tender. Stir occasionally with a fork to prevent the noodles from sticking to each other. Remove the pan from the heat. Drain the noodles in a colander, place them in a large mixing bowl and toss them in the remaining oil.

Place the noodles in a warmed serving dish and spoon the pork mixture over them. Serve immediately.

Stuffed Rigatoni

A surprisingly easy-to-make dish, Stuffed Rigatoni is a tasty way to serve pasta. As both the sauce and stuffing can be made well in advance, the final dish takes a very short time to prepare.

4 SERVINGS

Spaghetti alla Carbonara

SPAGHETTI WITH BACON AND EGG SAUCE

One of the great Italian pasta dishes, Spaghetti alla Carbonara is superb served with a green salad and lots of red wine.

4-6 SERVINGS

1½ oz. [3 tablespoons] butter
4 oz. lean bacon, rinds removed and chopped
3 tablespoons double [heavy] cream
3 eggs
4 oz. [1 cup] Parmesan cheese, grated
½ teaspoon salt
¼ teaspoon black pepper
1 lb. spaghetti, cooked for 10 to 12 minutes, drained and kept hot

In a small frying-pan, melt 1 tablespoon of the butter over moderate heat. When the foam subsides, add the bacon and cook, stirring occasionally, for 5 minutes or until it is crisp. Remove the pan from the heat and stir in the cream. Set aside.

In a medium-sized mixing bowl, beat the eggs and 2 ounces [½ cup] of the Parmesan cheese together with a fork until the mixture is smooth and the ingredients are well blended. Stir in the salt and pepper. Set aside.

Place the spaghetti in a large, deep serving bowl and add the remaining butter. Using two large spoons, toss the spaghetti until the butter has melted. Stir in the bacon mixture, tossing well. Finally, mix in the egg mixture, tossing and stirring until the spaghetti is well coated.

Serve at once, with the remaining grated cheese.

Spaghetti with Fennel Sauce

A fragrant mixture of fresh fennel, pine nuts, sultanas or seedless raisins and sardines combines to make this spaghetti a delicious dish.

4-6 SERVINGS

2 fl. oz. [¼ cup] olive oil
1 large onion, finely chopped
1 lb. canned sardines, drained
1 lb. fresh fennel, cooked, drained and finely chopped
1 tablespoon sultanas or seedless raisins
1 tablespoon blanched white pine nuts
8 fl. oz. [1 cup] dry white wine
½ teaspoon salt
1 teaspoon black pepper
1 lb. spaghetti, cooked for 10 to 12 minutes, drained and kept hot
4 oz. [1⅓ cups] dry white breadcrumbs, toasted and kept warm

In a medium-sized frying-pan, heat the olive oil over moderate heat. When the oil is hot, add the onion and sardines and fry, stirring occasionally, for 8 to 10 minutes or until the onion is golden.

Stir in the fennel, sultanas or seedless raisins and pine nuts. Add the wine, salt and pepper and bring the liquid to the boil. Reduce the heat to moderately low and simmer the sauce for 10 minutes, stirring frequently.

Place the spaghetti in a large, deep serving dish and pour over half of the sauce. Sprinkle over half of the breadcrumbs and, using two large spoons, toss the mixture until the spaghetti is thoroughly coated. Pour over the remaining sauce and top with the remaining breadcrumbs. Serve immediately.

Spaghetti with Meatballs and Tomato Sauce

Strictly speaking, Spaghetti with Meatballs and Tomato Sauce is more Italian-American than true Italian, though the Italians do have a passion for meatballs! Nearly every Italian-American cook has her own version of this dish — the main variations being in the composition of the meatballs. This recipe lays no claim to being the one and true original, but it can — and does — lay claim to being absolutely delicious and incredibly easy to eat. Serve as a main course with tossed green salad, garlic bread and lots of red wine.

4 SERVINGS

1 lb. spaghetti, cooked for 10 to 12 minutes, drained and kept hot
1 oz. [2 tablespoons] butter
4 oz. [1 cup] Parmesan cheese, grated

MEATBALLS

2 thick slices crusty bread, crusts removed
2 fl. oz. [¼ cup] milk
2 lb. lean minced [ground] beef
1 oz. [⅓ cup] fine dry breadcrumbs
1 oz. [¼ cup] Parmesan cheese, grated
1 egg, lightly beaten
½ teaspoon salt
½ teaspoon black pepper
1 teaspoon dried thyme
2 teaspoons grated lemon rind
1 large garlic clove, crushed
4 oz. [½ cup] butter

TOMATO SAUCE

2 oz. [¼ cup] butter
1 large onion, finely chopped
2 garlic cloves, crushed
1½ lb. canned Italian plum tomatoes
2½ oz. tomato purée
½ teaspoon salt
½ teaspoon freshly ground black pepper
½ teaspoon dried oregano

First make the meatballs. In a small bowl, soak the bread in the milk for 5 minutes, or until it has completely absorbed the liquid. Transfer the soaked bread to a large mixing bowl.

Add all the remaining meatball ingredients except the butter to the bowl and, using your hands, mix and knead the ingredients until they are well blended. Shape the mixture into about 30 walnut-sized balls. Place them on a baking sheet or aluminium foil and chill them in the refrigerator for 30 minutes.

Meanwhile, make the tomato sauce. In a large saucepan, melt the butter over moderate heat. When the foam subsides, add the onion and garlic and cook, stirring occasionally, for 5 to 7 minutes or until the onion is soft and translucent but not brown. Stir in the tomatoes with the can juice, the tomato purée, salt, pepper and oregano. Bring the liquid to the boil, stirring occasionally. Reduce the heat to low, cover the pan and simmer the sauce for 35 minutes.

Remove the meatballs from the refrigerator. In a large frying-pan, melt the butter over moderate heat. When the foam subsides, add the meatballs, a few at a time, and cook, carefully turning occasionally, for 6 to 8 minutes or until they are evenly browned. With a slotted spoon, remove the meatballs from the pan as they brown and set aside.

Carefully lower the meatballs into the tomato sauce and re-cover the pan. Continue to simmer for a further 20 to 30 minutes or until the meatballs are cooked.

Place the spaghetti in a large, deep serving dish and add the butter. Using two large spoons, toss the spaghetti until the butter has melted. Remove the pan containing the meatballs and sauce from the heat. Arrange the meatballs over the spaghetti, then pour over the sauce.

Sprinkle over half the Parmesan cheese and serve at once, with the remaining Parmesan cheese.

Serve immediately.

Three marvellous ways with spaghetti – Spaghetti alla Carbonara, Spaghetti with Meatballs and Tomato Sauce and Spaghetti with Fennel Sauce.

Sweet Noodle Pudding with Apples

A delightful but filling pudding, Sweet Noodle Pudding with Apples may be served with custard or cream.

4-6 SERVINGS

2 eggs, lightly beaten with 2 tablespoons milk
2 tablespoons sugar
¼ teaspoon salt
¼ teaspoon ground cinnamon
¼ teaspoon ground mixed spice or allspice
2 large cooking apples, peeled, cored and grated
2 oz. [⅓ cup] raisins
12 oz. fine noodles, cooked and drained
1 oz. [2 tablespoons] butter, melted

Preheat the oven to moderate 350°F (Gas Mark 4, 180°C).

In a large mixing bowl, combine the egg mixture, sugar, salt, cinnamon, mixed spice or allspice, apples, raisins and noodles. With a wooden spoon, stir the noodle mixture until the ingredients are

Noodles are a very versatile food—as you can see from this warming, filling dessert, Sweet Noodle Pudding with Apples.

well mixed.

Spoon the noodle mixture into a deep ovenproof dish and pour over the melted butter.

Place the dish in the oven and bake for 45 minutes or until the pudding is firm to the touch and lightly browned on top.

Remove the dish from the oven and serve the pudding immediately.

Tagliarini with Chicken Livers

This delightful and economical pasta dish may be served either as a first course or as a main dish, accompanied by a mixed green salad.

4-6 SERVINGS

2 tablespoons olive oil
1 lb. chicken livers, chopped
2 garlic cloves, crushed

1 lb. canned tomatoes, drained and with 4 fl. oz. [½ cup] of the can juice reserved
1 teaspoon salt
½ teaspoon black pepper
½ teaspoon dried thyme
½ teaspoon dried basil
6 oz. shelled peas
1 lb. tagliarini, cooked for 10 to 12 minutes and kept hot

In a flameproof casserole, heat the oil over moderate heat. Add the chicken livers and garlic and cook, stirring constantly, for 3 to 4 minutes or until the livers are lightly browned all over.

Add the tomatoes with the can juice, the salt, pepper, thyme and basil and bring the mixture to the boil, stirring. Reduce the heat to low and simmer for 30 minutes, stirring occasionally.

Add the peas and continue cooking, stirring occasionally, for a further 15 minutes. Remove the saucepan from the heat.

Place the tagliarini in a large serving bowl and pour over the sauce. Using two large spoons, toss the mixture until it is blended. Serve immediately.

Venetian Lasagne

 ① ☒ ☒

This pasta dish is perfect for a family supper. It needs no accompaniment other than a tossed mixed salad and some Chianti wine.

6-8 SERVINGS

- 2 fl. oz. [¼ cup] olive oil
- 1 lb. green lasagne
- 24 fl. oz. [3 cups] béchamel sauce
- 6 oz. [1½ cups] Parmesan cheese, grated

FILLING

- 2 oz. [¼ cup] butter
- 2 medium-sized onions, finely chopped
- 1 lb. uncooked chicken meat, finely minced [ground]
- 1 lb. lean veal, finely minced [ground]
- 1 oz. [¼ cup] flour
- 10 fl. oz. [1¼ cups] home-made chicken stock
- 1 teaspoon grated nutmeg
- 1 teaspoon salt
- 1 teaspoon freshly ground black pepper
- 8 oz. mushrooms, wiped clean and sliced
- 1 lb. leaf spinach, cooked and drained

3 tablespoons single [light] cream

First prepare the filling. In a large saucepan, melt the butter over moderate heat. When the foam subsides, add the onions and fry, stirring occasionally, for 5 to 7 minutes or until they are soft and translucent but not brown. Add the minced [ground] chicken and veal to the pan and fry, stirring occasionally, for 5 to 8 minutes or until the meat is lightly and evenly browned.

Stir in the flour, chicken stock, nutmeg, salt and pepper. Increase the heat to high and bring the liquid to the boil. Reduce the heat to low and simmer for 30 minutes, stirring occasionally. Add the mushrooms and spinach and simmer for another 30 minutes. Stir in the cream and remove the pan from the heat. Set the mixture aside while you cook the pasta.

Meanwhile, half-fill a large saucepan with water and add half of the olive oil. Bring the liquid to the boil over high heat.

Venetian Lasagne is a sustaining mixture of pasta, minced [ground] meat, mushrooms and spinach. Serve, as here, with red wine and salad for a really special family treat.

Reduce the heat to moderately high. Add half the lasagne to the pan, sheet by sheet, and cook it for 12 to 15 minutes or until it is 'al dente' or just tender. When the pasta is cooked, remove it from the pan with a fish slice or tongs, being careful not to tear the sheets. Set the sheets aside.

Add the remaining olive oil to the pan and cook the remaining lasagne in the same way.

Preheat the oven to moderate 350°F (Gas Mark 4, 180°C).

To assemble the lasagne, in a large lightly greased ovenproof casserole, make a layer of pasta. Cover it with a layer of the filling and then with alternating layers of béchamel sauce and Parmesan cheese. Continue making alternate layers of pasta, filling, béchamel sauce and Parmesan cheese, ending with a layer of lasagne sprinkled liberally with Parmesan cheese.

Place the casserole in the centre of the oven and cook the lasagne for 45 minutes to 1 hour. Remove the casserole from the oven.

To serve, cut the lasagne into approximately 3-inch squares and use a fish slice or tongs to remove them from the casserole. Serve the lasagne squares immediately.

Lasagne

A mouth-watering adaptation of the traditional Italian recipe, Lasagne is not for the conscientious weight-watcher! It is, however, quite definitely for those who love the warm rich taste of pasta. Lasagne need be accompanied only by a tossed green salad and a good hearty red wine — Barolo would be particularly appropriate. Cottage cheese may be substituted for the ricotta cheese if liked.

6-8 SERVINGS

2 fl. oz. [¼ cup] olive oil
1 lb. lasagne
1 lb. Mozzarella cheese, thinly sliced
1 lb. ricotta cheese
4 oz. [1 cup] Parmesan cheese, grated

SAUCE

2 fl. oz. [¼ cup] olive oil
2 large onions, finely chopped
2 garlic cloves, finely chopped
2 lb. lean minced [ground] beef
15 fl. oz. [1⅞ cups] tomato sauce (not tomato ketchup)
22 oz. canned peeled Italian tomatoes
2½ oz. tomato purée
4 fl. oz. [½ cup] water
1½ teaspoons salt
1 teaspoon black pepper
2 teaspoons sugar
1 teaspoon dried basil
2 bay leaves
8 oz. mushrooms, wiped clean and sliced

First, prepare the sauce. In a very large saucepan, heat the olive oil over moderate heat. When the oil is hot, add the onions and garlic and fry, stirring occasionally, for 5 to 7 minutes, or until the onions are soft and translucent but not brown. Add the beef to the pan and cook it for 5 to 8 minutes, stirring occasionally with a metal spoon, or until it is lightly and evenly browned.

Stir in the tomato sauce, tomatoes with the can juices, tomato purée, water, salt, pepper, sugar, basil and bay leaves. Bring the sauce to the boil. Reduce the heat to low and simmer the sauce for 2 hours, stirring occasionally.

Add the mushrooms and simmer for another hour.

Remove the pan from the heat and allow the sauce to cool to room temperature. With a metal spoon, skim off the fat from the surface of the sauce and discard the bay leaves. Transfer the sauce to a covered container and place it in the refrigerator overnight or until you are ready to assemble the lasagne.

Half fill a large saucepan with water and add half the olive oil. Bring the water to the boil over high heat. Add half of the lasagne to the pan, sheet by sheet, and cook it for 12 to 15 minutes, or until it is 'al dente' or just tender. When the pasta is cooked, remove it from the pan with a fish slice or tongs, being careful not to tear the sheets.

Add the remaining olive oil to the pan and cook the remaining lasagne in the same way. (The oil prevents the sheets of pasta from sticking together.)

Preheat the oven to moderate 350°F (Gas Mark 4, 180°C).

To assemble the lasagne, in a large ovenproof casserole make a layer of pasta. Cover it with a layer of meat sauce and then with alternating layers of mozzarella, ricotta and Parmesan cheese. Add another layer of pasta, then meat sauce and cheese. Continue adding alternative layers, ending with a layer of pasta sprinkled liberally with the Parmesan cheese.

Place the casserole in the oven and bake the lasagne for 1 hour. Remove the casserole from the oven.

To serve, cut the lasagne into 3-inch squares and use a fish slice to remove the portions from the casserole. Serve the lasagne squares immediately.

Mushroom and Bacon Lasagne

This is a more economical version of lasagne, since it requires only a little meat and omits some of the more expensive Italian cheeses used in the traditional recipe. It is marvellous, nevertheless — make a wonderful informal dinner by serving it with a mixed green salad and lots of smooth Chianti wine.

4 SERVINGS

3 tablespoons olive oil
6 oz. lasagne
15 fl. oz. double cream [1⅞ cups heavy cream], beaten until thick
4 oz. [1 cup] Parmesan cheese, grated

SAUCE

2 fl. oz. [¼ cup] vegetable oil
1 medium-sized onion, thinly sliced
1 garlic clove, crushed
1 carrot, scraped and chopped
1 celery stalk, trimmed and chopped
3 slices streaky bacon, rinds removed and chopped
6 oz. mushrooms, wiped clean and sliced
8 oz. lean beef, minced [ground]
¼ teaspoon dried oregano
¼ teaspoon dried basil

1 teaspoon salt
¼ teaspoon freshly ground black pepper
14 oz. canned peeled Italian tomatoes
3 tablespoons tomato purée
3 tablespoons single [light] cream

To prepare the sauce, in a large saucepan, heat the vegetable oil over moderate heat. When the oil is hot, add the onion, garlic, carrot and celery to the pan and cook, stirring occasionally, for 5 to 7 minutes, or until the onion is soft and translucent but not brown. Add the bacon and mushrooms and cook, stirring occasionally, for 5 minutes.

Add the meat to the pan and cook, stirring constantly, for 8 to 10 minutes, or until the meat is well browned. Stir in the oregano, basil, salt, pepper, tomatoes with the can juice and the tomato purée, mixing until the ingredients are well blended.

Reduce the heat to low, cover the pan and simmer the sauce, stirring occasionally, for 1 hour. If after an hour, the mixture is very liquid, remove the lid from the pan, increase the heat to moderate and cook for a further 15 minutes to evaporate

thinly sliced
1½ lb. canned peeled Italian
    tomatoes
2½ oz. tomato purée
1 teaspoon dried basil
½ teaspoon red pepper flakes
1 teaspoon salt
½ teaspoon freshly ground black
    pepper

First, prepare the sauce. In a medium-sized saucepan, heat the olive oil over moderate heat. When the oil is hot, add the onions and garlic and cook them, stirring occasionally, for 5 to 7 minutes, or until the onions are soft and translucent but not brown. Add the mushrooms to the pan and cook, stirring occasionally, for 3 to 5 minutes or until they are just tender.

Add the tomatoes with the can juice, the tomato purée, basil, red pepper flakes, salt and pepper and mix well to blend. Bring the liquid to the boil over moderately high heat, reduce the heat to low and simmer the sauce, stirring occasionally, for 40 minutes. Remove the pan from the heat and set aside while you cook the pasta.

Half fill a large saucepan with water and add 1 tablespoon of olive oil. Bring the water to the boil over high heat. Add half the lasagne to the pan, sheet by sheet, and cook it for 12 to 15 minutes or until it is 'al dente' or just tender. When the pasta is cooked, remove it from the pan with a fish slice or tongs, being careful not to tear the sheets.

Add the remaining olive oil to the pan and cook the remaining lasagne in the same way. (The oil prevents the sheets of pasta from sticking together.)

Preheat the oven to fairly hot 375°F (Gas Mark 5, 190°C).

Place one-third of the lasagne on the bottom of a medium-sized ovenproof casserole. Spread over half the cooked spinach and cover with half the mozzarella cheese. Pour over half of the tomato sauce and sprinkle over one-third of the Parmesan cheese. Continue to make layers in the same way until all the ingredients are used up, ending with a layer of lasagne sprinkled over with Parmesan cheese.

Place the casserole in the oven and bake the lasagne for 45 minutes. Remove the casserole from the oven and cut the lasagne into 3-inch squares.

Serve at once.

the excess liquid. Stir the cream into the sauce and remove the pan from the heat. Set aside.

Half fill a large saucepan with water and add 1 tablespoon of the olive oil. Bring the water to the boil over high heat. Add half the lasagne to the pan, sheet by sheet, and cook it for 12 to 15 minutes or until it is 'al dente' or just tender. When the pasta is done, remove it from the pan with a fish slice or tongs, being careful not to tear the sheets.

Add 1 tablespoon of the olive oil to the pan and cook the remaining lasagne in the same way. (The oil prevents the sheets of pasta from sticking together.)

Preheat the oven to moderate 350°F (Gas Mark 4, 180°C) and with a pastry brush, lightly brush a 2½-pound loaf tin with the remaining oil.

Place about one-third of the meat sauce mixture on the bottom of the tin. Pour over about one-third of the cream, then sprinkle over about one-quarter of the Parmesan cheese. Cover the mixture with a layer of one-third of the lasagne. Repeat these layers until all the ingredients are used up, finishing with a layer of Parmesan cheese.

Place the tin in the oven and cook for

40 minutes, or until the top is brown and bubbly. Remove the tin from the oven and cut into squares.

Serve at once.

Spinach Lasagne

☆ ☆   ①   ⋈ ⋈

With the substitution of spinach for meat, this version of lasagne makes a spicy and rich vegetarian meal. Serve it with a tomato and cucumber salad, lots of crusty bread and some well-chilled light white wine — a Toscano Bianco or a Frascati, for instance.

4-6 SERVINGS

2 tablespoons olive oil
6 oz. lasagne
3 lb. spinach, cooked
12 oz. Mozzarella cheese, thinly
    sliced
4 oz. [1 cup] Parmesan cheese,
    grated
SAUCE
2 fl. oz. [¼ cup] olive oil
2 medium-sized onions, thinly
    sliced
2 garlic cloves, crushed
4 oz. mushrooms, wiped clean and

Paglia e Fieno

PASTA WITH VEAL AND MUSHROOMS

Paglia e Fieno means literally 'straw and hay'. It is a rich dish which needs only a lightly tossed green salad and some garlic bread to make a delicious and sustaining supper for family or guests.

4-6 SERVINGS

2 oz. [¼ cup] plus 1 tablespoon
   butter
1 small onion, chopped
6 lean bacon slices, chopped
8 oz. veal, finely minced [ground]
½ teaspoon salt
¼ teaspoon black pepper
⅛ teaspoon dried oregano
1 lb. button mushrooms, wiped
   clean and sliced
8 fl. oz. single cream [1 cup light
   cream]
2 tablespoons finely chopped fresh
   parsley
6 oz. egg noodles, cooked for 5
   to 8 minutes, drained and kept
   hot
6 oz. green egg noodles, cooked

for 5 to 8 minutes, drained and
   kept hot
2 oz. [½ cup] Parmesan cheese,
   grated

In a medium-sized frying-pan, melt the 2 ounces [¼ cup] of butter over moderate heat. When the foam subsides, add the onion and bacon and cook, stirring occasionally, for 5 to 7 minutes or until the onion is soft and translucent but not brown.

Add the veal and cook, stirring constantly, for 5 minutes or until the veal is well browned. Stir in the salt, pepper, oregano and mushrooms and cook, stirring occasionally, for a further 5 minutes or until the mushrooms are tender.

Add the cream and parsley and stir well. Reduce the heat to low and cook the mixture, stirring occasionally, for a further 3 to 5 minutes or until it is hot but not boiling. Remove from the heat.

Colourful Pasta, Sausage and Bean Salad makes a nutritious 'scratch' meal. Serve with lots of red wine and crusty bread.

Place the noodles in a large serving dish. Add the remaining butter and, using two large spoons, toss the noodles.

Pour over the veal and mushroom mixture. Toss well and serve immediately, with the grated Parmesan cheese.

Pasta, Sausage and Bean Salad

An unusual and filling dish, Pasta, Sausage and Bean Salad is ideal to serve if unexpected guests drop in for supper (providing you have a well-stocked larder!) Lots of crusty French bread and butter and a bottle of red wine would be the ideal accompaniments.

6 SERVINGS

14 oz. canned French beans, halved
   and drained
 4 tomatoes, sliced
 8 oz. pork luncheon meat, diced
 2 medium-sized onions, sliced and
   pushed out into rings
14 oz. canned red kidney beans,
   drained

8 frankfurter sausages, cooked, drained, cooled and cut into ½-inch lengths

4 oz. [1 cup] black olives

8 oz. pasta shells, cooked, drained and cooled

1 small chorizo sausage, thinly sliced

½ cucumber, peeled and thinly sliced

4 oz. beetroots [beets], cooked, peeled and sliced

4 tablespoons chopped mustard and cress

DRESSING

1 teaspoon sugar

1 teaspoon salt

½ teaspoon black pepper

1 teaspoon prepared French mustard

1 garlic clove, crushed

2 fl. oz. [¼ cup] red wine vinegar

8 fl. oz. [1 cup] olive oil

Arrange the French beans in the bottom of a large salad bowl. Place the sliced tomatoes around the side of the bowl. Continue making layers with the luncheon meat, one of the onions, the kidney beans, frankfurter sausages, olives and half of the pasta shells. Cover the pasta shells with the remaining onion rings, the chorizo sausage, cucumber and beetroots [beets]. Cover the beetroots [beets] with the remaining pasta shells and the mustard and cress. Set aside.

In a small mixing bowl, combine all the dressing ingredients. Using a fork, beat the ingredients together until they are thoroughly combined.

Pour the dressing over the salad and serve immediately.

Sweetbreads with Pasta

This unusual and appetizing dish of sweetbreads and pasta may be served with grilled [broiled] tomatoes.

2-3 SERVINGS

1 lb. sweetbreads, soaked in cold water for 3 hours, drained, skinned and trimmed

2 oz. [½ cup] seasoned flour, made with 2 oz. [½ cup] flour, ½ teaspoon salt, ¼ teaspoon freshly ground black pepper and ½ teaspoon dried marjoram

2 oz. [¼ cup] butter

3 medium-sized carrots, scraped and thinly sliced

1 teaspoon dried thyme

1 bay leaf

4 fl. oz. [½ cup] Madeira

8 oz. macaroni, or other pasta, cooked and kept hot

Place the sweetbreads in a large saucepan and cover them with water. Place the pan over moderately high heat and bring the water to the boil. Remove the pan from

The unusual combination of taste and texture in Sweetbreads with Pasta makes it an exciting dish.

the heat and set the sweetbreads aside for 10 minutes.

Using a slotted spoon, remove the sweetbreads from the pan and drain them on kitchen paper towels. Discard the water. Place the sweetbreads on a board and cut them into ½-inch slices.

Put the seasoned flour on a plate. Dip the sweetbread slices in the flour, coating them thoroughly and shaking off any excess. Set aside.

In a large frying-pan, melt the butter over moderate heat. When the foam subsides, add the sweetbread slices and fry, turning occasionally, for 10 to 15 minutes or until they are lightly and evenly browned.

Using a slotted spoon, transfer the sweetbread slices to a plate and keep them hot.

Add the carrots, thyme, bay leaf and Madeira to the pan. Cook for 5 minutes, stirring frequently.

Add the macaroni to the pan, stirring until it is thoroughly coated with the sauce.

Remove the pan from the heat. Remove and discard the bay leaf. Spoon the mixture into a warmed serving dish. Arrange the sweetbread slices over the top and serve at once.

How to fill and cook Ravioli

Cut the 2 sheets of dough into circles with a 2-inch round, fluted pastry cutter. Using a teaspoon, place a portion of the filling mixture to be used in the centre of half of the dough circles. Using a pastry brush, draw a circle around the edge of each dough circle with a liberal quantity of water. Place the remaining dough circles on top of the filled dough circles and press firmly with your fingers around the edges to seal.

Cut the pasta sheets into rounds with a pastry cutter.

Place 1 teaspoon of the filling over half of the pasta rounds.

Moisten with water, place the remaining pasta rounds on top and seal.

To cook the ravioli, in a large saucepan, bring 3 to 4 pints [7½ to 10 cups] of water to the boil over high heat. Drop the ravioli into the boiling water and cook them, stirring occasionally with a wooden spoon, for 8 to 10 minutes or until the pasta is 'al dente' or just tender. With a slotted spoon, remove the ravioli from the pan and place them on a dampened cloth to drain.

Serve at once.

Ravioli di Manzo e Spinace

RAVIOLI FILLED WITH VEAL AND
SPINACH WITH TOMATO SAUCE

This delicious Italian dish is worth the time it takes to prepare. It makes a tasty and filling lunch or supper dish. For special occasions, serve it with a tossed mixed salad and lots of mellow Bardolino wine.

3-4 SERVINGS

SAUCE
2 tablespoons olive oil
1 medium-sized onion, finely chopped
2 lb. fresh tomatoes, blanched, peeled, seeded and chopped
14 oz. canned peeled Italian tomatoes
2½ oz. tomato purée
½ teaspoon dried basil
½ teaspoon dried oregano
1 teaspoon sugar
½ teaspoon salt
½ teaspoon freshly ground black pepper

FILLING
1 tablespoon butter
1½ tablespoons olive oil
1 small onion, finely chopped
2 garlic cloves, crushed
8 oz. lean veal, finely minced [ground]
6 oz. fresh spinach, cooked, drained and finely chopped
1 oz. [¼ cup] Parmesan cheese, finely grated
1 tablespoon double [heavy] cream
2 eggs, well beaten
¼ teaspoon grated nutmeg
¼ teaspoon salt
¼ teaspoon freshly ground black pepper

PASTA
8 oz. bought ravioli pasta, rolled out into 2 thin sheets

GARNISH
2 oz. [½ cup] Pecorino cheese, grated
1 tablespoon finely chopped fresh parsley

First make the tomato sauce. In a

Ravioli di Manzo e Spinace is a marvellous mixture of ravioli pasta filled with veal and spinach in a tomato sauce.

medium-sized saucepan, heat the oil over moderate heat. When the oil is hot, add the onion and fry, stirring occasionally, for 5 to 7 minutes or until it is soft and translucent but not brown. Stir in the fresh and canned tomatoes with the can juice, the tomato purée, basil, oregano,

54

sugar, salt and pepper, and bring to the boil. Reduce the heat to low, cover the pan and simmer the sauce, stirring occasionally, for 40 minutes or until it is very thick. Set aside.

Meanwhile, make the filling. In a large frying-pan, melt the butter with the oil over moderate heat. When the foam subsides, add the onion and garlic and fry, stirring occasionally, for 5 to 7 minutes or until the onion is soft and translucent but not brown. Add the meat to the pan and cook, stirring occasionally, for 8 to 10

minutes or until it is lightly browned. Add the spinach and, stirring frequently, cook for 5 to 8 minutes or until the juices have evaporated.

Remove the pan from the heat and transfer the meat and spinach mixture to a medium-sized bowl. Add the Parmesan, cream, eggs, nutmeg, salt and pepper and stir well to mix. The filling is now ready to use.

Fill, cook and drain the ravioli according to the instructions given in column one.

Preheat the grill [broiler] to moderately high.

Transfer the cooked ravioli to a warmed, flameproof serving dish and pour over the tomato sauce.

Sprinkle the Pecorino cheese over the tomato sauce and place the dish under the grill [broiler]. Grill [broil] for 5 minutes or until the cheese has melted and is golden.

Remove the dish from the heat, sprinkle over the parsley and serve the ravioli immediately.

Ravioli Piedmontese

RAVIOLI FILLED WITH BEEF AND
TOMATOES

*Ravioli Piedmontese is a very popular first
course to an Italian meal.*

6 SERVINGS

FILLING
2 oz. [¼ cup] butter
1 tablespoon vegetable oil
1 large onion, finely chopped
1 garlic clove, crushed
12 oz. lean beef, finely minced
   [ground]
8 fl. oz. [1 cup] beef stock
¼ teaspoon salt
½ teaspoon black pepper
8 oz. canned peeled tomatoes,
   coarsely chopped
1 teaspoon dried rosemary
½ teaspoon dried basil
2 oz. [½ cup] Parmesan cheese,
   finely grated

2 eggs, well beaten
PASTA
8 oz. bought ravioli pasta, rolled out
   into 2 thin sheets

To make the filling, in a large frying-pan,
melt the butter with the oil over moderate
heat. When the foam subsides, add the
onion and garlic and fry, stirring occasionally, for 8 to 10 minutes or until the
onion is golden brown. Add the beef and
fry, stirring occasionally, for 8 minutes
or until the meat is lightly browned.

Pour in the stock, and add the salt,
pepper, tomatoes with the can juice,
rosemary and basil to the beef. Cook the
mixture, stirring frequently, for 10
minutes or until the meat is cooked.

Remove the pan from the heat and
strain the contents through a fine wire
strainer held over a small saucepan. Set
the cooking liquid aside.

Put the contents of the strainer into a
mixing bowl. Add the Parmesan cheese

and eggs and stir the mixture until it is
thoroughly combined. The filling is now
ready to use.

Fill, cook and drain the ravioli according to the instructions given in column
one, page 54. While the ravioli is cooking,
heat the reserved cooking liquid over
moderate heat, stirring occasionally.

Transfer the drained ravioli to a
warmed serving dish, pour over the
cooking liquid and serve immediately.

Ravioli di Pisa

RAVIOLI FILLED WITH CHEESE,
SPINACH AND EGG WITH WALNUT SAUCE

*Ravioli di Pisa is a popular regional dish of
Italy.*

**Ravioli Piedmontese is pasta filled
with a beef and tomato mixture.**

SAUCE

6 oz. [1⅓ cups] walnuts, chopped

2 oz. [½ cup] cashew nuts, chopped

½ teaspoon dried oregano

¼ teaspoon salt

1 tablespoon water

4 oz. ricotta cheese

3 tablespoons olive oil

6 tablespoons single [light] cream

2 oz. [½ cup] Pecorino cheese, finely grated

4 fl. oz. [½ cup] milk

FILLING

2 oz. [¼ cup] butter

4 oz. fresh spinach, cooked, drained and finely chopped or 4 oz. frozen spinach, thawed and chopped

6 oz. ricotta cheese

2 hard-boiled eggs, chopped

¼ teaspoon salt

½ teaspoon black pepper

¼ teaspoon grated nutmeg

⅛ teaspoon ground saffron

PASTA

12 oz. bought ravioli pasta, rolled out into 2 thin sheets

First make the sauce. Place the walnuts, cashew nuts, oregano, salt and water in a mortar or small bowl. Using a pestle or fork, mash the ingredients to a smooth paste. Add the ricotta, olive oil and cream to the mixture and continue to mash until the mixture has a creamy texture. Stir in the Pecorino cheese and milk and transfer the mixture to a medium-sized saucepan.

Alternatively, blend the ingredients together in an electric blender. Place the pan over low heat and gently heat the sauce, stirring occasionally, until it is hot but not boiling. Remove the pan from the heat. Set aside and keep warm.

To make the filling, in a frying-pan melt the butter over moderate heat. When the foam subsides, add the spinach and cook for 4 minutes. Transfer the spinach to a plate. Set aside.

Put the ricotta in a bowl and mash it until it is smooth. Add the reserved spinach, eggs, salt, pepper, nutmeg and saffron and stir well to mix. The filling is now ready to use.

Fill, cook and drain the ravioli according to the instructions given in column one, page 54. Reheat the walnut sauce until it is hot. Transfer the ravioli to a warmed serving dish and pour over the walnut sauce. Stir them gently together and serve.

Ravioli di Pisa is pasta filled with a cheese mixture in walnut sauce.

Polish Ravioli

These little crescent shaped pasta, filled with a variety of sweet and savoury stuffings are the Polish version of ravioli. Serve them with a butter and breadcrumb sauce, as a first course, or with salad as a light meal.

4-6 SERVINGS

PASTA

12 oz. [3 cups] flour

1 teaspoon salt

3 large eggs, lightly beaten

2 to 3 tablespoons lukewarm water

FILLING

1 oz. [2 tablespoons] butter

1 onion, finely grated

1 lb. cream cheese

2 large egg yolks, beaten

½ teaspoon salt

¼ teaspoon black pepper

GLAZE

1 egg, beaten

1 teaspoon lukewarm water

First make the pasta. Sift the flour and salt into a mixing bowl. Make a well in the centre of the flour and pour in the lightly beaten eggs and water. With your fingertips, draw the flour into the liquid, until all the flour has been incorporated and the mixture forms a stiff dough.

Turn the dough out on to a lightly floured board and knead it for 10 minutes or until it is smooth but stiff.

Divide the dough in two and roll each piece out into a very thin sheet, pulling it with your hands into a rectangle.

Cover the sheets with a damp cloth and leave to rest for 30 minutes.

Meanwhile, prepare the filling. In a small frying-pan, melt the butter over moderate heat. When the foam subsides, add the grated onion and fry, stirring constantly, for 5 to 7 minutes, or until it is soft and translucent but not brown. Remove the pan from the heat and tip the contents into a mixing bowl.

Add the cream cheese to the onion and mix the ingredients well. Gradually beat in the egg yolks and salt and pepper until the mixture is smooth and creamy.

Uncover the dough sheets and, with a 3-inch pastry cutter, cut the dough into circles. Place one teaspoon of filling in the centre of each circle.

Combine the egg and the water for the glaze. Moisten the edges of the circles with this mixture. Fold the dough over the fillings to form semi-circles, and seal the edges by pressing them together.

In a large saucepan, bring 4 pints [5 pints] of salted water to the boil over high heat. Drop the circles into the water, cover and cook them for 6 to 15 minutes, depending on the thickness of the pasta, or until they are tender.

Remove the pan from the heat and drain the pasta in a colander. Transfer them to a warmed serving dish and serve.

Ravioli con Pollo

RAVIOLI FILLED WITH CHICKEN

Served with grated Parmesan cheese, this dish makes a delicious first course for an Italian meal or, accompanied by garlic bread and a full-bodied red wine, a filling main course.

2-4 SERVINGS

8 oz. bought ravioli pasta, rolled out into 2 thin sheets

SAUCE

2 tablespoons olive oil
1 small onion, finely chopped
1 garlic clove, finely chopped
1 celery stalk, trimmed and finely chopped
2 lb. canned peeled tomatoes, drained
1 teaspoon dried oregano
2 fl. oz. [¼ cup] red wine
¼ teaspoon salt
¼ teaspoon black pepper

FILLING

8 oz. cooked chicken meat, finely chopped
1 tablespoon grated Parmesan cheese
1 egg yolk, lightly beaten
⅛ teaspoon grated lemon rind
⅛ teaspoon grated nutmeg
⅛ teaspoon salt
⅛ teaspoon black pepper

First, make the sauce. In a medium-sized saucepan, heat the oil over moderate heat. When the oil is hot, add the onion, garlic and celery and fry, stirring occasionally, for 5 to 7 minutes or until the onion is soft and translucent but not brown.

Stir in the tomatoes, oregano, wine, salt and pepper and bring the mixture to the boil, stirring constantly. Reduce the heat to low and simmer the sauce for 40 minutes, stirring occasionally.

Meanwhile, place all the filling ingredients in a large mixing bowl and blend well with a wooden spoon. Set aside.

With a 2-inch round, fluted pastry cutter, cut the pasta dough into circles. Place half a teaspoon of the filling in the centre of each dough circle.

Using a pastry brush, moisten the edge of each dough circle with a liberal quantity of water. Fold the circles over to form semi-circles and press firmly around the edges to seal. Moisten the points of the ends of each semi-circle with a little water and press them together. Set aside.

In a large saucepan, bring about 4 pints

[5 pints] of water to the boil over high heat. Drop the pasta shapes into the boiling water and cook them, stirring occasionally with a wooden spoon, for 8 to 10 minutes or until the pasta is 'al dente' or just tender and they float to the top of the water.

With a slotted spoon, remove the pasta shapes from the pan and place them on a dampened cloth to drain.

Transfer the ravioli to a warmed serving dish and pour over the sauce. Serve immediately.

Rice Noodles with Pork and Prawns or Shrimps

An adaptation of a Thai dish, Rice Noodles with Pork and Prawns or Shrimps makes a simple one-dish meal or it may be served as part of a Thai meal. Traditionally, fish sauce, a salty mixture of crushed fermenting fish and salt is added to or served with many Thai dishes. Because fish sauce is not

Ravioli con Pollo is pasta filled with chicken in a tomato sauce. Serve as a first or main course.

always acceptable to Western taste soy sauce is suggested in its place. Rice noodles are available at Chinese delicatessens.

4-6 SERVINGS

1¼ teaspoons salt
1 lb. rice noodles
6 dried mushrooms, soaked in cold water for 20 minutes
4 tablespoons peanut oil
12 oz. pork fillets, cut into strips
8 oz. prawns or shrimps, shelled and weighed after shelling
6 spring onions [scallions], trimmed and finely sliced
1 garlic clove, crushed
½ teaspoon sugar
2 tablespoons fish sauce or soy sauce
1 tablespoon chopped fresh coriander leaves

Half-fill a large saucepan with water and add 1 teaspoon of salt. Set the pan over moderate heat and bring the water to the boil. Add the noodles and boil for 5 minutes. Drain the noodles and pour over 8 fluid ounces [1 cup] of cold water. Drain again. Place the drained noodles in a warmed serving dish and keep warm.

Remove the mushrooms from the water. Squeeze them dry and remove and discard the stems. Slice the mushrooms and set aside.

In a large frying-pan or wok, heat the oil over high heat. When the oil is very hot, reduce the heat to moderate. Add the pork strips and fry, stirring and turning constantly, for 2 to 3 minutes or until they are tender. Add the prawns or shrimps and fry, stirring constantly, for 2 to 3 minutes or until they turn pink. Add the spring onions [scallions], garlic and mushrooms and fry, stirring constantly, for 2 minutes. Stir in the sugar, fish or soy sauce and the remaining salt. Remove the pan from the heat.

Spoon the pork and prawn or shrimp mixture over the noodles. Garnish with the coriander leaves and serve.

Spaghetti all' Amatriciana
SPAGHETTI WITH BACON IN TOMATO SAUCE

A sumptuous Roman recipe, Spaghetti all' Amatriciana may be served with a mixed salad, crusty bread and wine.

4-6 SERVINGS

2 tablespoons olive oil
1 large onion, thinly sliced
2 garlic cloves, crushed
6 lean bacon slices, diced
2 fl. oz. [¼ cup] dry white wine
1 lb. canned peeled tomatoes, drained
½ teaspoon salt
1 teaspoon black pepper

½ teaspoon dried oregano
1 lb. spaghetti, cooked for 10 to 12 minutes, drained and kept hot
4 oz. [1 cup] Pecorino or Parmesan cheese, grated

In a saucepan, heat the oil over moderate heat. When the oil is hot, add the onion and garlic and fry, stirring occasionally, for 5 to 7 minutes or until the onion is soft and translucent but not brown.

Stir in the bacon and cook for a further 4 minutes, stirring constantly. Add the wine and bring the liquid to the boil. Boil rapidly for 2 minutes, then add the tomatoes. Stir in the salt, pepper and oregano and bring the liquid to the boil again.

Reduce the heat to moderately low and continue cooking for a further 15 minutes, stirring occasionally. Remove the pan from the heat.

Place the spaghetti in a large, deep serving dish and pour over the sauce. Using two large spoons, toss the mixture until the spaghetti is thoroughly coated with the sauce.

Sprinkle over the grated cheese and serve immediately.

Exotic Rice Noodles with Pork and Prawns or Shrimps from Thailand.

Spaghetti with Crabmeat

This is a pasta dish with a difference, since the crabmeat gives the spaghetti a rather exotic flavour. Serve it for a special dinner with a tossed green salad and, to drink, some well-chilled white Vouvray wine.

4 SERVINGS

2 oz. [¼ cup] butter
2 medium-sized onions, finely chopped
8 oz. mushrooms, wiped clean and sliced
8 oz. spaghetti, cooked for 10 to 12 minutes, drained and kept hot
8 oz. crabmeat, shell and cartilage removed
10 oz. canned condensed tomato soup
1 teaspoon salt
½ teaspoon black pepper
6 oz. [1½ cups] Parmesan cheese, grated
10 fl. oz. [1¼ cups] tomato juice

With 2 teaspoons of the butter, grease a

The perfect dish for a hungry family or friends—Tagliatelli Verdi with Bacon and Tomatoes. Serve with salad and crusty bread.

large, ovenproof casserole.

Preheat the oven to moderate 350°F (Gas Mark 4, 180°C).

In a medium-sized frying-pan, melt the remaining butter over moderate heat. When the foam subsides, add the onions and fry, stirring occasionally, for 4 minutes. Add the mushrooms and fry for a further 1 to 3 minutes or until the onions are soft and translucent but not brown. Remove the pan from the heat and set aside.

In a large mixing bowl, combine the mushroom and onion mixture with the spaghetti, crabmeat, soup, salt, pepper and 4 ounces [1 cup] of the cheese. Stir well to mix thoroughly, then pour in the tomato juice. Transfer the mixture to the prepared casserole and sprinkle over the remaining cheese.

Place the casserole in the oven and cook for 35 to 40 minutes or until the cheese is golden and bubbling.

Remove the casserole from the oven and serve at once.

Spaghetti con le Vongole
SPAGHETTI WITH CLAM SAUCE

Spaghetti con le Vongole is a delicious pasta dish from the Naples area. If clams are unobtainable, cockles or mussels may be substituted. Serve Spaghetti con le Vongole as a special light supper dish, accompanied by crusty bread and some well-chilled white wine.

4-6 SERVINGS

3 tablespoons olive oil
2 garlic cloves, crushed
1 tablespoon capers, finely chopped
1 medium-sized onion, finely chopped
1 lb. canned peeled tomatoes, drained
¼ teaspoon salt
½ teaspoon white pepper
1 teaspoon finely chopped fresh basil or ½ teaspoon dried basil
1 lb. canned clams, drained and chopped

1 tablespoon finely chopped fresh
parsley
1 lb. spaghetti, cooked for 10 to
12 minutes, drained and kept
hot
1 lemon, quartered

In a medium-sized saucepan, heat the oil over moderate heat. When the oil is hot, add the garlic, capers and onion and fry, stirring occasionally, for 5 to 7 minutes or until the onion is soft and translucent but not brown.

Stir in the tomatoes, salt, pepper and basil and bring the mixture to the boil, stirring constantly. Reduce the heat to low, cover the pan and simmer, stirring occasionally, for a further 30 minutes. Add the clams and the parsley and cook for a further 5 minutes or until the clams are heated through. Remove the pan from the heat.

Place the spaghetti in a large, deep serving dish and pour over the sauce. Using two large spoons, toss quickly until the spaghetti is thoroughly coated with the sauce.

Garnish with the lemon quarters and serve immediately.

Tagliatelli con Prosciutto
RIBBON PASTA WITH HAM

Tagiatelli con Prosciutto is a simple and delightful dish to serve either as a first or main course. Accompany it with plenty of hot garlic bread, a tossed, mixed green salad and lots of well-chilled white wine such as Soave.

4-6 SERVINGS

6 oz. [¾ cup] butter
12 oz. prosciutto, cut into 2-inch
strips
1 lb. tagliatelli, cooked for 8 to
10 minutes, drained and kept
hot
6 oz. [1½ cups] Parmesan cheese,
grated

In a medium-sized frying-pan, melt the butter over moderate heat. When the foam subsides, add the prosciutto and cook, stirring constantly, for 5 to 7 minutes or until it has heated through. Remove the pan from the heat and set it aside.

Place the tagliatelli in a large serving bowl and add the prosciutto and the butter remaining in the pan. Using two large spoons, toss the mixture until all the tagliatelli strands are thoroughly coated with the butter.

Sprinkle over the cheese and serve immediately.

Tagliatelli Verdi with Bacon and Tomatoes

This easy-to-make and inexpensive dish may be served as a first course or, with a tossed mixed green salad and crusty bread, as a scrumptious main course for lunch or supper.

4-6 SERVINGS

1 oz. [2 tablespoons] plus 1 teaspoon
butter
8 streaky bacon slices, rinds
removed and very coarsely
chopped
1 medium-sized onion, finely
chopped
2 large garlic cloves, finely
crushed
8 oz. small button mushrooms,
wiped clean and halved
6 medium-sized tomatoes,
blanched, peeled and coarsely
chopped
1½ teaspoons salt
1 teaspoon freshly ground black
pepper
1 tablespoon finely chopped fresh
tarragon or 1½ teaspoons dried
tarragon
1 teaspoon chopped fresh oregano
or ½ teaspoon dried oregano
10 fl. oz. [1¼ cups] béchamel sauce
4 fl. oz. double cream [½ cup heavy
cream]
4 oz. [1 cup] Parmesan cheese,
grated
1 lb. tagliatelli verdi, cooked
for 8 to 10 minutes, drained
and kept hot
3 tablespoons dry white
breadcrumbs
1 tablespoon melted butter

Preheat the oven to fairly hot 375°F (Gas Mark 5, 190°C). Using the teaspoon of butter, grease a large, deep-sided baking dish and set it aside.

In a large, heavy-based saucepan, fry the bacon over moderately high heat for 6 to 8 minutes or until it has rendered all of its fat. Scrape the bottom of the pan frequently with a spatula to prevent the bacon from sticking.

Using a slotted spoon, remove the bacon from the pan and set it aside on a plate. Add the remaining butter to the pan and reduce the heat to moderate. When the foam subsides, add the onion and garlic and fry, stirring occasionally, for 8 to 10 minutes or until the onion is golden brown. Add the mushrooms and fry, stirring frequently, for 3 minutes. Stir in the chopped tomatoes, salt, pepper, tarragon, oregano, béchamel sauce, cream, and 3 ounces [¾ cup] of the Parmesan cheese. Cook the mixture, stirring constantly, for 3 minutes.

Remove the pan from the heat and add the reserved bacon and the tagliatelli to the mixture. Using two large spoons, stir well to coat the mixture thoroughly with the sauce.

Spoon the mixture into the prepared baking dish and set aside.

In a small mixing bowl, combine the remaining cheese with the breadcrumbs and melted butter. Sprinkle the mixture over the tagliatelli mixture and place the dish in the centre of the oven. Bake for 30 minutes or until the top is deep golden brown.

Remove the dish from the oven and serve the tagliatelli immediately, straight from the dish.

Tagliatelli Verdi con Salsa di Tonno
GREEN RIBBON PASTA IN TUNA FISH SAUCE

A simple and colourful pasta dish, Tagliatelli Verdi con Salsa di Tonno is a good 'emergency' meal since most of the ingredients can be kept in the store cupboard. Serve as either a first or main course and accompany it with brown bread and butter and, to drink, some well-chilled white wine, such as Soave.

4-6 SERVINGS

2 fl. oz. [¼ cup] olive oil
12 oz. canned tuna fish, drained and
flaked
2 tablespoons finely chopped fresh
parsley
14 fl. oz. [1¾ cups] home-made
chicken stock
1½ teaspoons freshly ground black
pepper
1 lb. tagliatelli verdi, cooked
for 8 to 10 minutes, drained
and kept hot
1 tablespoon butter

In a medium-sized frying-pan, heat the oil over moderate heat. When the oil is hot, reduce the heat to low and add the tuna fish and 1½ tablespoons of the parsley.

Cook, stirring constantly with a wooden spoon, for 5 minutes, then add the stock and black pepper. Continue cooking for a further 5 minutes, stirring from time to time.

Place the tagliatelli in a large serving bowl and add the butter. Using two large spoons, toss the tagliatelli until all the strands are thoroughly coated with the butter. Pour over the sauce and sprinkle with the remaining parsley.

Serve immediately.

Vermicelli Soup

An easily digestible and nourishing soup, Vermicelli Soup is very quick and easy to make once you have prepared the basic chicken stock. This soup is ideal to serve to invalids.

6-8 SERVINGS

3 pints [7½ cups] home-made chicken stock
½ teaspoon salt
1 teaspoon chopped fresh lemon thyme
6 oz. vermicelli
1 tablespoon lemon juice

In a medium-sized saucepan, bring the chicken stock, salt and lemon thyme to the boil over high heat. Add the vermicelli, reduce the heat to moderately low and cook, stirring frequently, for 3 to 5 minutes or until the vermicelli is 'al dente' or just tender. Stir in the lemon juice.

Remove the pan from the heat and pour the soup into a warmed soup tureen. Serve immediately.

Vermicelli and Vegetables Chinese-Style

Quick to make, easy to eat — Vermicelli and Vegetables Chinese-Style is the perfect supper dish for a working wife or mother. Serve with ice-cold lager or some well-chilled Moselle wine.

4 SERVINGS

3 oz. [⅜ cup] butter
1 medium-sized onion, finely chopped
1 garlic clove, crushed
1 large green pepper, white pith removed, seeded and finely chopped
3 celery stalks, trimmed and chopped
2 carrots, scraped and thinly sliced
4 Chinese mushrooms, soaked for 20 minutes in cold water, drained and chopped
8 oz. bean sprouts
4 water chestnuts, sliced
4 oz. canned pineapple chunks, drained and chopped and with 6 fl. oz. [¾ cup] of the can juice reserved
1 tablespoon white wine vinegar

Two superb—and very different— dishes using vermicelli: Vermicelli Soup and Vermicelli and Vegetables Chinese-Style.

½ teaspoon salt
½ teaspoon black pepper
¼ teaspoon cayenne pepper
1½ tablespoons soy sauce
1 lb. vermicelli

In a large saucepan, melt the butter over moderate heat. When the foam subsides, add the onion, garlic, green pepper, celery and carrots and cook, stirring occasionally, for 5 to 7 minutes or until the onion is soft and translucent but not brown. Stir in the mushrooms, bean sprouts, water chestnuts and pineapple chunks and stir to mix well. Pour over the reserved pineapple can juice and vinegar, and add the salt, pepper, cayenne and soy sauce. Bring the liquid to the boil, stirring occasionally. Stir in the vermicelli, reduce the heat to low and simmer the mixture, stirring occasionally, for 3 to 5 minutes or until the vermicelli is 'al dente' or just tender and the vegetables are cooked through.

Remove the pan from the heat and transfer the mixture to a warmed serving dish.

Serve at once.

Wonton Dough

This recipe is for the basic dough used to make wonton wrappers. The dough is rolled out very thinly — not more than $\frac{1}{16}$-inch thick — then cut to the required shapes, filled and cooked.

1 POUND [4 CUPS] DOUGH

1 lb. [4 cups] flour
2 teaspoons salt
2 eggs, lightly beaten with 3 fl. oz. [⅜ cup] water

Sift the flour and salt into a large mixing bowl. Make a well in the centre and pour in the egg mixture. Using your fingers or a spatula, draw the flour into the liquid. When all the flour has been incorporated and the dough comes away from the sides of the bowl, turn the dough on to a lightly floured surface and knead it vigorously for 10 minutes or until it is smooth and elastic.

The dough is now ready to use.

Wontons with Pork and Prawns or Shrimps

These deep-fried wontons are deliciously crunchy and make a marvellous meal served with steamed rice and a salad.

4 SERVINGS

2 tablespoons vegetable oil

8 oz. lean pork, minced [ground]
8 oz. peeled prawns or shrimps, finely chopped
2 tablespoons soy sauce
1 tablespoon dry sherry
½ teaspoon salt
5 canned bamboo shoots, drained and finely chopped
2 Chinese mushrooms, washed, soaked in cold water for 20 minutes, drained and finely chopped
2 spring onions [scallions], trimmed and finely chopped
1 teaspoon cornflour [cornstarch] mixed with 1 tablespoon water or dry sherry
8 oz. wonton dough, thinly rolled and cut into 36 x 3-inch squares, or 36 bought wonton wrappers sufficient vegetable oil for deep frying

In a large frying-pan, heat the oil over high heat. When the oil is hot, reduce the heat to moderately high. Add the pork and fry, stirring constantly, for 1 minute or until the meat begins to brown. Add the prawns or shrimps, soy sauce, sherry, salt, bamboo shoots, mushrooms and spring onions [scallions] and fry, stirring constantly, for a further 1 minute. Add the cornflour [cornstarch] mixture to the pan and stir until the liquid thickens. Remove the pan from the heat and, using a large spoon, transfer the mixture to a bowl. Set aside to cool.

Place the wonton wrappers on a flat working surface. Place a teaspoon of the filling just below the centre of each wrapper. Using a pastry brush dipped in water, wet the edges of the dough. Fold one corner of the dough over the filling to make a triangle and pinch the edges together to seal. Pull the corners at the base of the triangle together and pinch them to seal. As each wonton is ready, place it on a plate. Repeat this process until all the wontons wrappers are filled and sealed.

Fill a large deep-frying pan one-third full with vegetable oil. Set the pan over moderate heat and heat the oil until it reaches 375°F on a deep-fat thermometer or until a small cube of stale bread dropped into the oil turns golden brown in 40 seconds.

Add the wontons to the oil, 8 or 10 at a time, and fry for 2 minutes or until they are golden brown. With a slotted spoon, remove the wontons from the oil and drain them on kitchen paper towels. Keep hot while you fry and drain the remaining wontons in the same way.

Transfer the wontons to a heated serving dish and serve at once.

Zite with Meatballs and Tomato Mushroom Sauce

Serve Zite with Meatballs and Tomato Mushroom Sauce as a main meal with lots of crusty bread, green salad and red wine.

4 SERVINGS

1 teaspoon salt
1 lb. zite
MEATBALLS
1½ lb. beef or pork, minced [ground]
2 slices white bread, soaked in
    4 tablespoons milk for 5 minutes
2 teaspoons grated lemon rind
2 oz. [⅔ cup] dried breadcrumbs
1 large egg
2 garlic cloves, crushed
1 teaspoon salt
1 teaspoon black pepper
1½ teaspoons dried oregano
2 fl. oz. [¼ cup] olive oil
8 oz. Italian sausages, chopped
SAUCE
3 tablespoons olive oil
1 large onion, thinly sliced
2 garlic cloves, crushed
4 oz. mushrooms, sliced
4 oz. fresh peas
28 oz. canned peeled tomatoes

6 fl. oz. [¾ cup] red wine
5 oz. tomato purée
½ teaspoon salt
1 teaspoon black pepper
1 teaspoon dried oregano
4 oz. Mozzarella cheese, thinly
    sliced

First make the meatballs. In a mixing bowl, combine all the ingredients except the oil and sausages, beating until they are well mixed. Shape the mixture into walnut-sized balls. Place the balls in a large plate and chill them in the refrigerator for 30 minutes.

Meanwhile, make the sauce. In a saucepan, heat the oil over moderate heat. When the oil is hot, add the onion and garlic and fry, stirring occasionally, for 5 to 7 minutes or until the onion is soft and translucent but not brown. Add the mushrooms and peas and fry for 3 minutes. Add the tomatoes with the can juice, the wine, purée, salt, pepper and oregano and stir to mix. Bring the liquid to the boil over moderate heat. Reduce the heat to low, cover the pan and simmer the sauce for 30 minutes. Remove from the heat.

In a large frying-pan, heat the oil over

Zite with Meatballs and Tomato Mushroom Sauce—fabulous to eat!

moderate heat. When the oil is hot, add the meatballs, a few at a time, and fry, turning occasionally, for 5 to 8 minutes or until they are lightly and evenly browned. Transfer the cooked meatballs to the saucepan containing the sauce. Brown the remaining meatballs and the sausage pieces in the same way. Return the saucepan to low heat and simmer the mixture for a further 30 minutes.

Add the cheese slices to the pan and continue to simmer for a further 10 to 15 minutes or until the cheese has melted.

Meanwhile, half-fill a saucepan with water and add the salt. Set the pan over moderately high heat and bring the water to the boil. When the water boils, add the zite to the pan. Reduce the heat to moderate and cook the zite for 10 to 15 minutes or until it is 'al dente' or just tender. Remove the pan from the heat and drain the zite in a colander.

Transfer the zite to a large serving bowl. Remove the pan of sauce and meatballs from the heat. Pour the mixture over the zite and serve.